The Wild Side
In the Line of Duty

The Wild Side
In the Line of Duty

Henry Billings
Melissa Billings

JAMESTOWN  PUBLISHERS

a division of NTC/CONTEMPORARY PUBLISHING GROUP
Lincolnwood, Illinois USA

ISBN 0–8092-9829-5

Published by Jamestown Publishers,
a division of NTC/Contemporary Publishing Group, Inc.,
4255 West Touhy Avenue,
Lincolnwood (Chicago), Illinois 60712, U.S.A.
© 2001 NTC/Contemporary Publishing Group, Inc.

7 8 9 10 11 12 113 09 08 07 06

Hayden McGinley

CONTENTS

UNIT THREE

To the Student

Many people work in dangerous professions. People such as firefighters, pilots, and nurses often risk their lives in the line of duty.

The articles in this book are all about people who found themselves in dangerous work situations. Some are about people who risked their own lives to save other people. Others are about accidents that happened on the job. You will probably learn something from every article. You will come away from some of them amazed at what people can endure. You will be touched or horrified by others. But you will not be bored.

As you read and enjoy the 15 articles in this book, you will be developing your reading skills. If you complete all the lessons in this book, you will surely increase your reading speed and improve your reading comprehension and critical thinking skills. Also, because the exercises following the articles include items of the types often found on state and national tests, learning how to complete them will prepare you for tests you may have to take in the future.

How to Use This Book

About the Book.   *In the Line of Duty* contains three units, each of which includes five lessons. Each lesson begins with an article about someone in a dangerous situation in the line of duty. The article is followed by a group of four reading comprehension exercises and three critical thinking exercises. The reading comprehension exercises will help you understand the article. The critical thinking exercises will help you think about what you have read and how it relates to your own experience.

At the end of each lesson, you will also have the opportunity to give your personal response to some aspect of the article and then to assess how well you understood what you read.

The Sample Lesson.   Working through the sample lesson, the first lesson in the book, with your class or group will demonstrate how a lesson is organized. The sample lesson explains how to complete the exercises and score your answers. The correct answers for the sample exercises and sample scores are printed in lighter type. In some cases, explanations of the correct answers are given. The explanations will help you understand how to think through these question types.

If you have any questions about how to complete the exercises or score them, this is the time to get the answers.

Working Through Each Lesson.   Begin each lesson by looking at the photograph and reading the caption. Before you read, predict what you think the article will be about. Then read the article.

Sometimes your teacher may decide to time your reading. Timing helps you keep track of and increase your reading speed. If you have been timed, enter your reading time in the box at the end of the lesson. Then use the Words-per-Minute Table to find your reading speed, and record your speed on the Reading Speed Graph at the end of the unit.

Next complete the Reading Comprehension and Critical Thinking exercises. The directions for each exercise will tell you how to mark your answers. When you have finished all four Reading Comprehension exercises, use the answer key provided by your teacher to check your work. Follow the directions after each exercise to find your score. Record your Reading Comprehension scores on the graph at the end of each unit. Then check your answers to the Author's Approach, Summarizing and Paraphrasing, and Critical Thinking exercises. Fill in the Critical Thinking Chart at the end of each unit with your evaluation of your work and comments about your progress.

At the end of each unit you will also complete a Compare and Contrast Chart. The completed chart will help you see what the articles have in common, and it will give you an opportunity to explore your own ideas about the events in the articles.

SAMPLE LESSON

Fire In Midair

On March 31, 1998, England's Leeds United soccer team lost a match by a score of 3–0. So the players weren't very happy as they rode in the bus to the airport. But soon they weren't thinking about the defeat at all. They were thinking about how grateful they were to be alive.

2   The team was 50 minutes late getting to the airport. It was after midnight before everyone was settled into his or her seat. Captain John Hackett and the rest of the flight crew were busy preparing the plane for flight. During this time, one of the

The fire-damaged engine can be seen on the plane that was carrying England's Leeds United soccer team when the plane had to make an emergency landing.

passengers thought he smelled airplane fuel. He mentioned it to the person sitting in the seat beside him. No one else seemed to notice anything, however. Finally, at 12:20 A.M., Captain Hackett steered the plane down the runway. In a moment, the 67-foot turboprop plane, with 44 people on board, was airborne.

3   The plane climbed quickly. In just a few seconds it was 150 feet off the ground. Its speed was up to 140 miles per hour. Then, without any warning, the right engine caught fire. Before long, it was completely engulfed in flames.

4   Captain Hackett did not know about the fire right away. His instruments did not show any trouble. He found out only when a crew member entered the cabin and told him. Meanwhile, the flight attendants rushed to calm the passengers. They also told them to prepare for a crash landing.

5   When the passengers saw the flames, they screamed in terror.

6   "Fire!" yelled some. "There's a fire!"

7   Others hollered, "Stop! Stop!"

8   But this was a plane, not a car. Captain Hackett couldn't just put on

the brakes. Still, Hackett had to find a way to land the plane in a hurry. The flaming right engine could explode at any moment.

9   Hackett knew what he was supposed to do. Safety rules stated clearly what should be done in such an emergency. He was supposed to circle the runway. Only then could he land. But Hackett didn't think he had enough time to do that. So he tried something bolder.

10   The runway at the airport was long. Looking down, Hackett saw that the plane was flying over the last part of it. He had to make a split-second decision. Hackett turned the nose of the plane toward the ground. He knew the only chance of anyone surviving this crash was if he could land the plane on whatever bit of runway was left.

11   Hackett brought the plane down fast. When it landed, it bounced hard several times. Then it rolled off the end of the runway, its nose plowing into the grass. The plane skidded for 100 yards and stopped just before hitting a fence. The plane's nose was buried in the ground and its tail hung in the air.

12 The passengers were desperate to get off the plane. They knew it might still explode at any time. David O'Leary, the soccer team's assistant manager, was sitting near an exit door. He tried to open it, but it was stuck. O'Leary rammed the door with his shoulder. It flew open. Quickly, he helped people off the plane. Meanwhile the crew opened the two other exits. Because of the plane's awkward position, some people had to jump a long way to the ground. Some sprang from the wing, others from the tail.

13 Although it took about 30 seconds to get everyone off the plane safely, it probably seemed like hours. People were clamoring to get out, but those near the exits knew they should wait. They wanted to make sure they weren't going to leap into the flames.

14 After one player watched his teammates jump from the plane, it was his turn. "I thought for a moment I couldn't do it," he said. When he jumped and rolled over, everyone shouted to him to get away from the plane. No one knew whether or not the aircraft was going to blow up. "I'm lucky to be alive," he said.

15 With the plane's right engine still burning, the passengers scurried to the airport building. A fire crew, wearing special suits, worked quickly to put out the fire.

16 Both passengers and crew agreed that Captain Hackett was a hero. He had done the right thing in landing immediately. To circle the airport for a proper landing would have taken 8 or 10 minutes. There was a strong possibility that a wing would have caught fire. Or fuel leaking from the engine could have caused another explosion. That would have meant certain death for every person on board.

17 Thanks to the quick thinking of Captain Hackett, everything turned out all right. To Hackett himself, however, it was all in the line of duty. He didn't see himself as a hero. "I think any other pilot would have reacted the same way," he said.

If you have been timed while reading this article, enter your reading time below. Then turn to the Words-per-Minute Table on page 55 and look up your reading speed (words per minute). Enter your reading speed on the graph on page 56.

Reading Time: Sample Lesson

_____ : _____
Minutes   Seconds

A | Finding the Main Idea

One statement below expresses the main idea of the article. One statement is too general, or too broad. The other statement explains only part of the article; it is too narrow. Label the statements using the following key:

M—Main Idea   **B—Too Broad**   **N—Too Narrow**

_B_   1. Airline pilots may break the rules and land when they want to if they think it is necessary. [This statement is too broad. The article is about a particular incident. It does not mention why the crash landing was necessary.]

_N_   2. In March 1998 a turboprop plane carrying 44 people caught fire. [This statement is too narrow. It tells only one part of the story.]

_M_   3. An airline pilot made a split-second decision to attempt a crash landing when he discovered his plane was on fire. [This is the main idea. It tells what happened in the article. It also tells why it happened.]

_15_	Score 15 points for a correct M answer.
_10_	Score 5 points for each correct B or N answer.
_25_	**Total Score:** Finding the Main Idea

B | Recalling Facts

How well do you remember the facts in the article? Put an X in the box next to the answer that correctly completes each statement about the article.

1. The right engine of the plane caught fire as the plane
   ☒ a. climbed to 150 feet.
   ☐ b. descended to 150 feet.
   ☐ c. leveled out at 150 feet.

2. Captain Hackett didn't know about the fire right away because
   ☐ a. no one told him.
   ☒ b. his instruments did not show any trouble.
   ☐ c. he did not hear the shouting.

3. Captain Hackett did not circle the runway before landing because he
   ☐ a. had lost control of the plane.
   ☐ b. was following the safety rule for emergencies.
   ☒ c. did not think he had enough time.

4. Captain Hackett's plan was to bring the plane down
   ☒ a. on the last section of runway.
   ☐ b. on the roof of the airport.
   ☐ c. in an open field.

5. After pushing the door open, O'Leary
   ☐ a. jumped from the wing and ran to the airport building.
   ☐ b. shouted at people near the exits to wait.
   ☒ c. helped people off the plane.

	Score 5 points for each correct answer.
_25_	**Total Score:** Recalling Facts

C Making Inferences

When you combine your own experience with information from a text to draw a conclusion that is not directly stated in that text, you are making an inference. Below are five statements that may or may not be inferences based on information in the article. Label the statements using the following key:

C—Correct Inference   **F—Faulty Inference**

___F___ 1. Turboprop planes are more likely than other planes to have an emergency. [This is a *faulty* inference. There is nothing to indicate that the emergency was related to the style of the plane.]

___C___ 2. Captain Hackett's emergency landing was dangerous and could have killed everyone on board. [This is a *correct* inference. The article states that the landing did not follow standard safety procedures.]

___F___ 3. There is no need to learn emergency rules because every emergency situation is different. [This is a *faulty* inference. The fact that the emergency rules were not followed in this case does not imply that they are not generally useful.]

___F___ 4. If Captain Hackett had circled the runway before landing, the plane would have crashed. [This is a *faulty* inference. We do not know what would have happened if Captain Hackett had circled the runway.]

___C___ 5. If the passenger that smelled fuel had alerted the flight attendant, the emergency probably would have been avoided. [This is a *correct* inference. You can infer that if Captain Hackett had known about the fuel smell, he would not have taken off.]

Score 5 points for each correct answer.

___25___ **Total Score:** Making Inferences

D Using Words Precisely

Each numbered sentence below contains an underlined word or phrase from the article. Following the sentence are three definitions. One definition is closest to the meaning of the underlined word. One definition is opposite or nearly opposite. Label those two definitions using the following key; do not label the remaining definition.

C—Closest   **O—Opposite or Nearly Opposite**

1. Before long, it was completely <u>engulfed</u> in flames.

_____ a. melted

___C___ b. swallowed up

___O___ c. barely burned

2. Because of the plane's <u>awkward</u> position, some people had to jump a long way to the ground.

___O___ a. good

_____ b. final

___C___ c. hard to manage

3. The passengers were <u>desperate</u> to get off.

___C___ a. needing greatly

___O___ b. calmly waiting

_____ c. sorry

4. People were <u>clamoring</u> to get out.

___O___ a. asking permission

_____ b. standing

___C___ c. demanding noisily

5. With the plane's right engine still burning, the passengers <u>scurried</u> to the airport building.

_C_   a. ran quickly

_O_   b. strolled

_____   c. entered

    _15_   Score 3 points for each correct C answer.

    _10_   Score 2 points for each correct O answer.

    _25_   **Total Score:** Using Words Precisely

Enter the four total scores in the spaces below, and add them together to find your Reading Comprehension Score. Then record your score on the graph on page 57.

Score	Question Type	Sample Lesson
_25_	Finding the Main Idea	
_25_	Recalling Facts	
_25_	Making Inferences	
_25_	Using Words Precisely	
_100_	**Reading Comprehension Score**	

Author's Approach

Put an X in the box next to the correct answer.

1. The main purpose of the first paragraph is to

☒ a.   show how unprepared for adventure the players were.

☐ b.   describe why the soccer players were unhappy and tired.

☐ c.   show that losing a soccer game is not so bad.

2. From the statements below, choose the one that you believe the authors would agree with.

☐ a.   Since the plane did not explode, the passengers did not need to exit in a hurry.

☒ b.   Everyone on the plane reacted sensibly in the face of danger.

☐ c.   The passengers should have left the plane from the exits closer to the ground.

3. Choose the statement below that best describes the authors' position in paragraph 14.

☐ a.   One passenger's fear of jumping was less than his fear of fire.

☐ b.   One passenger overcame his fear in the face of danger.

☒ c.   One person's experience was likely shared to some degree by all the passengers.

4. What do the authors mean by the statement "[Captain Hackett's] instruments did not show any trouble"?

☒ a.   The instruments were not working properly.

☐ b.   The instruments were not designed to indicate fire.

☐ c.   The instruments were working fine, even though the wing was on fire.

    _4_   Number of correct answers

Record your personal assessment of your work on the Critical Thinking Chart on page 58.

Summarizing and Paraphrasing

Follow the directions provided for question 1. Put an X in the box next to the correct answer for question 2.

1. Complete the following one-sentence summary of the article using the lettered phrases from the phrase bank below. Write the letters on the lines.

Phrase Bank

a. Captain Hackett's decision to try an emergency landing

b. a description of how the passengers made it to safety

c. a description of the events before takeoff

The article about the emergency landing begins with ___c___,

goes on the describe ___a___, and ends with ___b___.

2. Read the statement from the article below. Then read the paraphrase of that statement. Choose the reason that best tells why the paraphrase does not say the same thing as the statement.

Statement: In extreme cases, airline pilots must break the rules of safety, especially when human life is in danger.

Paraphrase: Airline pilots may break the rules of safety whenever they see the need.

☐ a. Paraphrase says too much.

☐ b. Paraphrase doesn't say enough.

☒ c. Paraphrase doesn't agree with the statement from the article.

___2___ Number of correct answers

Record your personal assessment of your work on the Critical Thinking Chart on page 58.

Critical Thinking

Put an X in the box next to the correct answer for questions 1, 3, 4, and 5. Follow the directions provided for question 2.

1. Which of the following statements from the article is an opinion rather than a fact?

☐ a. The team was 50 minutes late getting to the airport.

☒ b. Although it took about 30 seconds to get everyone off the plane safely, it probably seemed like hours.

☐ c. A fire crew, wearing special suits, worked quickly to put out the fire.

2. Choose from the letters below to correctly complete the following statement. Write the letters on the lines.

In the article, ___a___ and ___c___ are alike.

a. Captain Hackett's decision to land the plane

b. the flight attendants' decision to calm the passengers

c. David O'Leary's decision to ram the exit door with his shoulder

3. What did you have to do to answer question 2?

☐ a. find a cause (why something happened)

☒ b. find a comparison (how things are the same)

☐ c. draw a conclusion (a sensible statement based on the text and your experience)

4. What was the effect of the plane landing with its tail high in the air?

☐ a. Some people were seriously injured.

☐ b. The fire on the right engine got worse.

☒ c. Some people had to jump from high off the ground to exit the plane.

5. If the attendants had not prepared the passengers for a crash landing, you can predict that

☐ a. many of the passengers would have been injured or killed.

☒ b. the passengers would probably have survived anyway, since the plane was only about 150 feet off the ground.

☐ c. the passengers would have been able to get to the exits faster.

___5___ Number of correct answers

Record your personal assessment of your work on the Critical Thinking Chart on page 58.

Personal Response

I know how David O'Leary felt when he couldn't get the emergency exit open because _____

_____ [Write about an experience you had in which you had to overcome a physical

barrier by force.]

_____

_____

Self-Assessment

From reading this article, I have learned _____

_____ [Explain any facts or lessons you have learned from reading this article.]

_____

_____

_____

Self-Assessment

To get the most out of the *Wild Side* series, you need to take charge of your own progress in improving your reading comprehension and critical thinking skills. Here are some of the features that help you work on those essential skills.

Reading Comprehension Exercises. Complete these exercises immediately after reading each article. They help you recall what you have read, understand the stated and implied main ideas, and add words to your working vocabulary.

Critical Thinking Skills Exercises. These exercises help you focus on the author's approach and purpose, recognize and generate summaries and paraphrases, and identify relationships between ideas.

Personal Response and Self-Assessment. Questions in this category help you relate the articles to your personal experience and give you the opportunity to evaluate your understanding of the information in that lesson.

Compare and Contrast Charts. At the end of each unit you will complete a Compare and Contrast chart. The completed chart helps you see what the articles have in common and gives you an opportunity to explore your own ideas about the topics discussed in the articles.

The Graphs. The graphs and charts at the end of each unit enable you to keep track of your progress. Check your graphs regularly with your teacher. Decide whether your progress is satisfactory or whether you need additional work on some skills. What types of exercises are you having difficulty with? Talk with your teacher about ways to work on the skills in which you need the most practice.

UNIT ONE

Into the Flames

Smoke jumpers fight a fire deep in the forest.

You don't have to be crazy, but it helps. This old joke is often used to describe people who do dangerous work. A test pilot would be one example. So, too, would a race car driver. But it is hard to think of a more hazardous job than smoke jumping.

2   A want ad for smoke jumpers might read like this. "Wanted: A few brave souls who enjoy jumping out of a plane to reach and put out forest fires. Must be willing to land on a steep slope or high up in a tree. Applicants must not be afraid of raging fire or choking smoke. Must be able to cut trees and dig trenches for

hours on end. In fact, must be willing to work for days straight without rest. Must also be able to hike miles through the wilderness while carrying a 100-pound pack. And, oh yes, the pay is lousy."

3   Jumping out of a plane into a fire has always been risky work. Smoke jumpers knew that. But on August 5, 1949, they learned just how deadly their job could be. At 12:25 that afternoon, a fire broke out about 20 miles north of Helena, Montana. It happened in a place called Mann Gulch. The day was hot, dry, and windy. That meant the fire would spread quickly. Mann Gulch was deep in the wilderness. It was far from any roads. So this was clearly a job for smoke jumpers.

4   Fifteen smoke jumpers answered the call. They climbed onto a plane and flew to the gulch. At 3:30 P.M. they parachuted into the woods. The jump didn't go well. High winds forced the men to jump higher than they had planned. As a result, they landed far apart. It took them more than an hour to find each other.

5   Still, that didn't seem like a big deal at the time. The fire looked routine. "I took a look at the fire and decided it wasn't bad. . . . I thought it probably wouldn't burn much more that night," said one.

6   Because the fire didn't look bad, the group took their time getting organized. Their leader's name was R. Wagner "Wag" Dodge. As Dodge gathered the men together, he heard someone shouting near the fire. It was Jim Harrison, a forest ranger. Harrison had been the first to see the fire. He had been trying to fight it alone for hours. Dodge left the group to speak with Harrison. At 5:40 P.M., he and Harrison rejoined the crew. The men were now ready to put out the fire.

7   They all headed down the gulch toward the Missouri River. But just then the fire flared up below them. This was no routine fire after all. It was a killer.

8   Powerful winds fed the flames. These flames leaped as high as 200 feet. Temperatures in the blaze soared to 1,800 degrees. Now the men realized their mistake. They should have put out the fire when they had the chance. But it was too late to worry about that now. The fire was closing in on them. It was moving up the slope at a furious speed.

9   Quickly, Dodge ordered his men to turn around and go back up the gulch. He hoped they could make it up over the ridge line and down the other side before the fire overtook them. That seemed to be their only hope. The men dropped their gear and ran as fast as they could. It was a race against death. The odds were not good. Forest fires spread faster going up a hill than down. But the men could not run very fast up the steep incline.

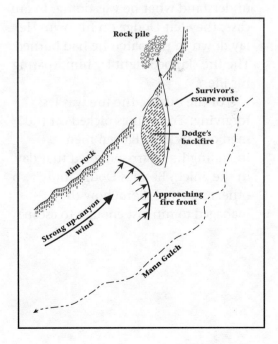

10   As they scrambled up the slope, Wag Dodge had another idea. Suddenly he stopped and lit a backfire. This technique was new at the time. The goal was to burn a patch of ground before the main fire could reach it. The fire would move around such a patch because there would be nothing left to burn inside it. By lying down inside the burned-out area, a firefighter could save his or her life.

11   As Dodge lit his backfire, he called to the other men. He wanted them to wait with him and join him in the burned-out patch. They refused. Perhaps they thought they could outrun the fire. Or perhaps they didn't understand what he was doing. In any case, they left Dodge on his own. He lay down in the patch he had burned. The fire skipped right by him, sparing his life.

12   For the others, the fire was less forgiving. The flames picked off the men one by one. Eleven men, including Jim Harrison, died that day in the gulch. Besides Dodge, only two others survived. Somehow they managed to run fast enough to escape the flames. Two other men made it out but died from their burns the next day.

13   The country was shocked and saddened by the deaths of the smoke jumpers. Some good did come out of the tragedy, however. For one thing, it showed how unpredictable a fire can be. A tiny blaze can turn into a raging inferno. The Mann Gulch fire also proved the wisdom of starting a backfire. That is a standard technique today.

14   Beyond that, the fire showed that smoke jumpers needed more and better equipment. Wag Dodge's crew had just one two-way radio. It got smashed during the jump. So the men had no way to talk to the outside world. Today a smoke jumping crew will carry several radios.

15   Clothing has also come a long way. In 1949 the men wore jeans and cotton, long-sleeved work shirts. They wore baseball caps. Today all smoke jumpers wear fire-resistant clothes. They wear hard hats. Every smoke jumper carries a small rolled-up shelter. It is made from aluminum that doesn't burn. This shelter can come in handy if a fire gets too close. A person can open it up and crawl inside. Then he or she can wait for the fire to pass by.

16   Today's smoke jumpers also follow 10 strict rules. Everyone carries a copy of these rules inside his or her hard hat. One rule is to "establish lookouts." Another is to "know your safety zones and escape routes."

17   Still, smoke jumping remains dangerous. It's a job that saves lives, forests, and property. But it's not for everyone. After all, only a few people would fit the description in that want ad.

If you have been timed while reading this article, enter your reading time below. Then turn to the Words-per-Minute Table on page 55 and look up your reading speed (words per minute). Enter your reading speed on the graph on page 56.

Reading Time: Lesson 1

_____ : _____
Minutes   Seconds

A | Finding the Main Idea

One statement below expresses the main idea of the article. One statement is too general, or too broad. The other statement explains only part of the article; it is too narrow. Label the statements using the following key:

M—Main Idea   **B—Too Broad**   **N—Too Narrow**

_____ 1. Smoke jumping is dangerous work.

_____ 2. Thirteen people died in the Mann Gulch fire of 1949.

_____ 3. The fire in Mann Gulch in 1949 showed how dangerous smoke jumping could be, and why better equipment was needed.

> _____ Score 15 points for a correct M answer.
>
> _____ Score 5 points for each correct B or N answer.
>
> _____ **Total Score:** Finding the Main Idea

B | Recalling Facts

How well do you remember the facts in the article? Put an X in the box next to the answer that correctly completes each statement about the article.

1. Smoke jumpers were sent into Mann Gulch because
   - [ ] a. the day was hot, dry, and windy.
   - [x] b. it was in the wilderness and far from any roads.
   - [x] c. a fire had started.

2. The smoke jumpers in Mann Gulch took their time getting organized because
   - [ ] a. the fire didn't look bad.
   - [x] b. they didn't know what to do.
   - [x] c. they landed far apart.

3. Dodge lit a backfire because he thought
   - [ ] a. it would stop the fire from spreading.
   - [x] b. he could outrun the fire.
   - [x] c. it could save his life.

4. From the Mann Gulch fire, people learned that
   - [x] a. starting a backfire is a good technique.
   - [x] b. being a smoke jumper is dangerous.
   - [x] c. blue jeans were not fire-resistant.

5. Today, smoke jumpers wear
   - [x] a. aluminum suits.
   - [x] b. blue jeans and workshirts.
   - [x] c. fire-resistant clothes and hard hats.

> Score 5 points for each correct answer.
>
> _____ **Total Score:** Recalling Facts

C | Making Inferences

When you combine your own experience with information from a text to draw a conclusion that is not directly stated in that text, you are making an inference. Below are five statements that may or may not be inferences based on information in the article. Label the statements using the following key:

C—Correct Inference   F—Faulty Inference

_____ 1. Smoke jumping is not a popular job.

_____ 2. It isn't important to put out a routine fire right away.

_____ 3. Mann Gulch was the first fire in which smoke jumpers died.

_____ 4. Fires spread more quickly in hot weather.

_____ 5. In 1949, most of the smoke jumpers did not know about backfires.

Score 5 points for each correct answer.

_____ **Total Score**: Making Inferences

D | Using Words Precisely

Each numbered sentence below contains an underlined word or phrase from the article. Following the sentence are three definitions. One definition is closest to the meaning of the underlined word. One definition is opposite or nearly opposite. Label those two definitions using the following key; do not label the remaining definition.

C—Closest   O—Opposite or Nearly Opposite

1. But it is hard to think of a more <u>hazardous</u> job than smoke jumping.

_____ a. safe

_____ b. exciting

_____ c. dangerous

2. "Applicants must not be afraid of <u>raging</u> fire or choking smoke."

_____ a. uncontrolled

_____ b. mild

_____ c. burning

3. The fire looked <u>routine</u>.

_____ a. weak

_____ b. typical

_____ c. unusual

4. Temperatures in the blaze <u>soared</u> to 1,800 degrees.

_____ a. rose quickly

_____ b. reached

_____ c. dropped

5. The fire skipped right by him, <u>sparing</u> his life.

_____ a. taking

_____ b. saving

_____ c. protecting

Enter the four total scores in the spaces below, and add them together to find your Reading Comprehension Score. Then record your score on the graph on page 57.

Score	Question Type	Lesson 1
_____	Finding the Main Idea	
_____	Recalling Facts	
_____	Making Inferences	
_____	Using Words Precisely	
_____	**Reading Comprehension Score**	

Author's Approach

Put an X in the box next to the correct answer.

1. The authors use the first sentence of the article to

☐ a. entertain the reader.

☐ b. get the reader's attention.

☐ c. describe smoke jumpers.

2. What do the authors mean by the statement, "But some good did come out of the tragedy"?

☐ a. It is good to experience tragedy.

☐ b. From the tragedy, people learned how to make smoke jumping safer.

☐ c. The smoke jumpers were good people.

3. What is the authors' purpose in writing "Into the Flames"?

☐ a. to inform the reader about the Mann Gulch fire

☐ b. to explain what smoke jumpers do

☐ c. to persuade the reader to become a smoke jumper

_____ Number of correct answers

Record your personal assessment of your work on the Critical Thinking Chart on page 58.

Summarizing and Paraphrasing

Follow the directions provided for question 1. Put an X in the box next to the correct answer for questions 2 and 3.

1. Look for the important ideas and events in paragraphs 8 and 9. Summarize those paragraphs in one or two sentences.

_____

_____

_____

_____

2. Below are summaries of the article. Choose the summary that says all the most important things about the article but in the fewest words.

☐ a. Smoke jumping can be deadly, as people found out at Mann Gulch in 1949.

☐ b. Poor equipment and delays in organizing at Mann Gulch in 1949 turned a routine smoke jump into a tragedy that resulted in better techniques and equipment for smoke jumpers.

☐ c. Because of windy weather, poor equipment, and delays in getting organized, a fire in Mann Gulch in 1949 got out of control. The smoke jumpers tried to outrun it, but only three survived. From the tragedy, people learned how important it was to set backfires and to have better equipment.

3. Choose the best one-sentence paraphrase for the following sentence from the article: "The flames picked off the men one by one."

☐ a. All the men were killed by the flames.

☐ b. The flames killed the men one by one.

☐ c. One by one, the men escaped the flames.

_____ Number of correct answers

Record your personal assessment of your work on the Critical Thinking Chart on page 58.

Critical Thinking

Put an X in the box next to the correct answer for questions 1, 2, 4, and 5. Follow the directions provided for question 3.

1. Which of the following statements from the article is an opinion rather than a fact?

☐ a. Jumping out of a plane into a fire has always been risky work.

☐ b. Forest fires spread faster going up a hill than down.

☐ c. Perhaps they thought they could outrun the fire.

2. From the article, you can predict that

☐ a. no smoke jumpers have died since 1949.

☐ b. fewer smoke jumpers die on the job now than in the past.

☐ c. there are more smoke jumpers now than in the past.

3. Using what you know about smoke jumping from the article, list at least two ways that it is similar now to the way it was in 1949, and two ways that it is different.

Similarities

_____

_____

_____

Differences

_____

_____

_____

4. What was the effect of the smoke jumpers taking a long time to get organized to fight the fire?

☐ a. The fire became worse.

☐ b. Wag Dodge lit a backfire.

☐ c. The jump didn't go well.

5. Into which of the following theme categories would this article best fit?

☐ a. a day on the job

☐ b. lessons learned from tragedy

☐ c. firefighting, past and present

_____ Number of correct answers

Record your personal assessment of your work on the Critical Thinking Chart on page 58.

Personal Response

What was most surprising or interesting to you about this article?

_____

_____

_____

_____

Self-Assessment

From reading this article, I have learned _____

_____

_____

_____

_____

Doctors (and Nurses) Without Borders

Mary Lightfine knew the old man was dying. She washed him and gave him some fresh blankets to keep him warm. Then she found a tent where he could lie down. But there was nothing more she could do. Lightfine felt terrible for him. She said, "I kept thinking . . . what a horrible feeling to be dying in a refugee camp."

2 Lightfine was right. It was very sad for the man to die in such grim conditions. But it would have been even worse if Lightfine had not been there to help. She was part of a group called Doctors Without Borders. On this day in 1997, she was in a refugee

Kosovars in a refugee camp in Macedonia wait in line for medical service.

camp in Macedonia. She was there to help war victims from nearby Kosovo.

3 Doctors Without Borders began in the 1970s. It was started by French doctors. They wanted to give medical care to those who needed it most. That included people in remote parts of the world. It included those who lived through natural disasters. It also included victims of war. The doctors knew it was risky to go to some of these places. But they believed everyone should have medical care, no matter where they lived.

4 By the 1990s Doctors Without Borders had become a worldwide group. It had about 2,000 workers in more than 80 countries. These workers came from 45 different nations. They weren't paid for their services. They were volunteers. One of the volunteers was Mary Lightfine.

5 Lightfine had had a quiet childhood. She spent many of her early years on a farm in Ohio. So she knew how to feed hens and clean out barns. When she grew up, she wanted more action in her life. So she became an emergency room nurse.

6 For 16 years Lightfine worked in emergency rooms across the United States. By 1992 she felt ready for a change. She still wanted to help the sick and needy. But she wanted to travel more. She wanted to see other countries and learn about other ways of life. When a friend suggested Doctors Without Borders, Lightfine decided to give it a try.

7 It was a decision that changed her life. Over the next eight years, Lightfine worked for Doctors Without Borders in 10 different countries. She gave children vaccines in Uganda. She handed out food in Sudan. She stitched up wounds in Macedonia.

8 Along the way, Lightfine saw a lot of suffering. On the day she bathed the dying man, she also comforted a woman whose home had been destroyed by war. She bandaged a child who had been hurt in the fighting. "If I move fast and don't think about it, I'll be able to perform my work," she said.

9 Sometimes, though, she could barely believe what she saw. She treated one man who had been beaten by enemy soldiers. Said Lightfine, "From his waist down [he] was blue like a gym bag. He had been tortured

and beaten. In all the emergencies I have worked, I have never seen any person bruised that much. It was very difficult for me to imagine that someone could do that to another person."

10   It was not just the physical wounds that were hard to look at. Lightfine also saw people in great emotional pain. Some had lost their homes. Others had seen family members killed. Many feared their lives would never return to normal. "Sometimes the most important thing I do is hold their hand," Lightfine said.

11   With children, Lightfine often gave out markers. She had them draw pictures. She found that was a good way for them to express their feelings. Many drew burning houses or soldiers with guns. Some even made drawings of people being killed.

12   On most days Lightfine was at work by 7 A.M. Often she did not stop until midnight. Even when she did have some free hours, she had no place to relax. Her living space was not exactly plush.

13   In Nicaragua, for instance, Lightfine lived in a tiny house along with several others. "It's very basic," she wrote at the time. "There's no stove or refrigerator, and we're eating only canned food. I'm sleeping on a mat on the floor of a windowless pantry."

14   Lightfine went on to describe the heat. She wrote, "It's so hot here that even sleeping with one sheet and a fan on is uncomfortable. I don't have a thermometer, but it must be near 100 degrees."

15   In Sudan things were even worse. Some of the time she lived in a pup tent. The rest of the time she slept in a mud shelter. Lightfine was the only human in the shelter. But there were plenty of rats to keep her company.

16   Given the hardships, it may seem surprising that Lightfine loved her job. But she did. She liked helping people. Beyond that, she found that the people she treated were always very grateful. Some were so thankful they cried. Others hugged her or gave her special blessings.

Some tried to share their last bit of food with her. In Macedonia one woman threw her arms around Lightfine and kissed her. Said Lightfine, "More people have said thank you here than in 10 years of working in an emergency room back home. When people say thank you, you've made a difference. For me, that is the greatest gift."

If you have been timed while reading this article, enter your reading time below. Then turn to the Words-per-Minute Table on page 55 and look up your reading speed (words per minute). Enter your reading speed on the graph on page 56.

Reading Time: Lesson 2

_____ : _____
Minutes   *Seconds*

A Finding the Main Idea

One statement below expresses the main idea of the article. One statement is too general, or too broad. The other statement explains only part of the article; it is too narrow. Label the statements using the following key:

M—Main Idea   **B—Too Broad**   **N—Too Narrow**

_____ 1. The group Doctors Without Borders gives medical care to victims of war or natural disasters.

_____ 2. In spite of the hardships she experienced, nurse Mary Lightfine found her work with the group Doctors Without Borders rewarding.

_____ 3. In 1997, nurse Mary Lightfine worked in a refugee camp in Macedonia.

_____ Score 15 points for a correct M answer.

_____ Score 5 points for each correct B or N answer.

_____ **Total Score:** Finding the Main Idea

B Recalling Facts

How well do you remember the facts in the article? Put an X in the box next to the answer that correctly completes each statement about the article.

1. Doctors Without Borders was started by
   ☐ a. Mary Lightfine.
   ☐ b. a group of French doctors.
   ☐ c. a worldwide organization.

2. Mary Lightfine became an emergency room nurse because she
   ☐ a. wanted to travel more.
   ☐ b. didn't like farm work.
   ☐ c. wanted more action in her life.

3. The people who work for Doctors Without Borders
   ☐ a. are well paid.
   ☐ b. come from more than 80 countries.
   ☐ c. see a lot of suffering.

4. Lightfine did _not_ help people
   ☐ a. who needed vaccines.
   ☐ b. rebuild their homes.
   ☐ c. who were in emotional pain.

5. According to the story, Lightfine did _not_ live in
   ☐ a. an apartment.
   ☐ b. a mud shelter.
   ☐ c. a pup tent.

Score 5 points for each correct answer.

_____ **Total Score:** Recalling Facts

C Making Inferences

When you combine your own experience with information from a text to draw a conclusion that is not directly stated in that text, you are making an inference. Below are five statements that may or may not be inferences based on information in the article. Label the statements using the following key:

C—Correct Inference   **F—Faulty Inference**

_____ 1. People who work for Doctors Without Borders must be doctors or nurses.

_____ 2. Many remote areas have no doctors.

_____ 3. Volunteers with Doctors Without Borders choose what countries they want to go to.

_____ 4. Mary Lightfine's family did not approve of her work.

_____ 5. Volunteers with Doctors Without Borders live in conditions similar to those of the people they are helping.

Score 5 points for each correct answer.

_____ **Total Score:** Making Inferences

D Using Words Precisely

Each numbered sentence below contains an underlined word or phrase from the article. Following the sentence are three definitions. One definition is closest to the meaning of the underlined word. One definition is opposite or nearly opposite. Label those two definitions using the following key; do not label the remaining definition.

C—Closest   **O—Opposite or Nearly Opposite**

1. It was very sad for the man to be dying in such <u>grim</u> conditions.

_____ a. dirty

_____ b. awful

_____ c. pleasant

2. That meant people in <u>remote</u> spots.

_____ a. far away

_____ b. poor

_____ c. close by

3. The doctors knew it was <u>risky</u> to go to such places.

_____ a. safe

_____ b. frightening

_____ c. dangerous

4. Her living space was not exactly <u>plush</u>.

_____ a. fancy

_____ b. plain

_____ c. big

5. Given the <u>hardships</u>, it may seem surprising that Lightfine loved her job.

_____ a. comforts

_____ b. living conditions

_____ c. difficulties

_____ Score 3 points for each correct C answer.

_____ Score 2 points for each correct O answer.

_____ **Total Score:** Using Words Precisely

Enter the four total scores in the spaces below, and add them together to find your Reading Comprehension Score. Then record your score on the graph on page 57.

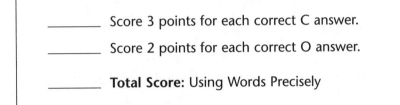

Score	Question Type	Lesson 2
_____	Finding the Main Idea	
_____	Recalling Facts	
_____	Making Inferences	
_____	Using Words Precisely	
_____	**Reading Comprehension Score**	

Author's Approach

Put an X in the box next to the correct answer.

1. The main purpose of the first paragraph is to

☐ a. introduce the topic of the article.

☐ b. describe the old man who was dying.

☐ c. entertain the reader.

2. What is the authors' purpose in writing "Doctors (and Nurses) Without Borders"?

☐ a. to describe the conditions in refugee camps

☐ b. to describe Mary Lightfine

☐ c. to inform the reader about the group Doctors Without Borders

3. Choose the statement below that best describes the authors' position in paragraph 16.

☐ a. Working for Doctors Without Borders is difficult.

☐ b. In spite of the hardships, working for Doctors Without Borders is very rewarding.

☐ c. People in the United States are not grateful for the medical help they receive.

_____ Number of correct answers

Record your personal assessment of your work on the Critical Thinking Chart on page 58.

Summarizing and Paraphrasing

Follow the directions provided for the questions below.

1. Reread paragraph 9 in the article. Below, write a summary of the paragraph in no more than 25 words.

_____

_____

_____

Reread your summary and decide whether it covers the important ideas in the paragraph. Next, decide how to shorten the summary to 15 words or less without leaving out any essential information. Write this summary below.

_____

_____

_____

2. Complete the following one-sentence summary of the article using the lettered phrases from the phrase bank below. Write the letters on the lines.

> ## Phrase Bank
> a. a description of a refugee camp in Macedonia
> b. what the organization is
> c. an explanation of why one volunteer liked her work

The article about Doctors Without Borders begins with _____,

goes on to explain _____, and ends with _____.

3. Read the statement from the article below. Then read the paraphrase of that statement. Choose the reason that best tells why the paraphrase does not say the same thing as the statement.

Statement: Many feared their lives would never return to normal.

Paraphrase: Many were afraid they would never be able to return home.

☐ a. Paraphrase says too much.

☐ b. Paraphrase doesn't say enough.

☐ c. Paraphrase doesn't agree with the statement from the article.

> _____ Number of correct answers
>
> Record your personal assessment of your work on the Critical Thinking Chart on page 58.

Critical Thinking

Follow the directions provided for questions 1, 3, and 5. Put an X in the box next to the correct answer for questions 2 and 4.

1. For each statement below, write *O* if it expresses an opinion or *F* if it expresses a fact.

_____ a. "I kept thinking . . . what a horrible feeling to be dying in a refugee camp."

_____ b. She wanted to see other countries and learn about other ways of life.

_____ c. Given the hardships, it may seem surprising that Lightfine loved her job.

2. From what the article told you about Mary Lightfine, you can predict that

☐ a. she will continue working for Doctors Without Borders.

☐ b. she is no longer working for Doctors Without Borders.

☐ c. there will not be much need for people with Lightfine's skills in the future.

3. Choose from the letters below to correctly complete the following statement. Write the letters on the lines.

According to paragraph 5, _____ because _____.

   a.   she had had a quiet childhood

   b.   Mary Lightfine became an emergency room nurse

   c.   she wanted more action in her life

4. Because of Mary Lightfine's work

☐ a. her life was uninteresting.

☐ b. she loved her job.

☐ c. many people were helped.

5. Which paragraphs provide evidence from the article to support your answer to question 4?_____

_____ Number of correct answers

Record your personal assessment of your work on the Critical Thinking Chart on page 58.

Personal Response

A question I would like to ask Mary Lightfine is _____

_____

_____

_____

_____

Self-Assessment

I can't really understand how _____

_____

_____

_____

_____

Bass Reeves: Hero of the Wild West

Bass Reeves searched for outlaws in towns such as this one, which is a ghost town today.

If you were an outlaw in the Old West, you knew one thing for sure. You didn't want Bass Reeves on your trail. This U.S. deputy marshal almost always got his man. From 1875 to 1907 he tracked down outlaws in what is now the state of Oklahoma. During these years, Reeves captured more than 3,000 criminals. Bass Reeves was one of the best lawmen in the Wild West.

2 No one could have predicted such a future for Reeves. He was born a slave in 1838. He grew into a tall,

strong adult. One day in the early 1860s, he quarreled with his master. A fight broke out between them. Reeves hit his master and knocked him out. Under slave laws, that was a major crime. Reeves knew he could be put to death for striking a white man. So he fled across the Red River to Oklahoma. He lived with the Indians of that region for several years.

3   In 1865 slavery was abolished. Ten years after that, Reeves became a marshal. He was appointed by Judge Isaac Parker. Parker's court was in Fort Smith, Arkansas. But the judge also ruled over Oklahoma. This was the most lawless part of the Old West. It was so bad that some people said, "There is no God west of Fort Smith."

4   Parker knew how wild the region was. All kinds of outlaws hid out there. Among them were train robbers, horse thieves, and killers. Parker wanted these outlaws brought to justice. So he appointed 200 marshals to track them down. One of these marshals was Bass Reeves.

5   Reeves got the job in part because he knew the region well. He knew where the best hideouts were. He knew the likely escape routes. Also, he could speak the languages of the local Indians. So he could turn to them for help when he needed it. In addition, Reeves was good with a gun. He was so good, in fact, that his friends wouldn't let him join their shooting contests because they knew he would always win.

6   Still, being a marshal was a risky job. Many outlaws were ready to fight to the death. Marshals were often killed in shootouts. Others were killed in ambushes. Like all marshals, Bass Reeves was a marked man. Outlaws wanted very much to see him dead. Many times they shot at him. But they always missed. They never even wounded him.

7   Reeves was, of course, lucky. But he was also very smart. He knew it was safer to sneak up on outlaws than make a direct charge at them. And Reeves was a master of disguise. He often posed as a cowboy or farmer. Outlaws often didn't know who he was until he snapped the handcuffs on them.

8   Once Reeves went after two young outlaws near the Texas border. He heard they were hiding at their mother's home. So he decided to pay them a visit. But he didn't go dressed as a U.S. marshal. Instead, he dressed up as a tramp. He put on an old floppy hat. To make it look authentic, Reeves shot three holes in it. He left his horse at a camp 28 miles away. Then he made the long, hot walk to the mother's house.

U.S. Marshal Bass Reeves

9   By the time he got there, he was tired and dirty. He really did look like a tramp. Reeves knocked on the door. He begged the mother for a bite to eat, telling her how hungry he was. He said his feet hurt from walking so far. He also mentioned that marshals were after him and had nearly killed him. He took off his hat and showed her the three bullet holes.

10   The mother took pity on Reeves. She invited him in. She gave him food and began chatting with him. She told him about her two outlaw sons. She even suggested that he might join them in a life of crime.

11   Later the mother heard a whistle. It came from her sons. They had been hiding during the day and wanted to know if it was safe to return home. The mother signaled back that all was clear. When the sons appeared, the mother introduced them to Reeves. They agreed to let him join their gang.

12   With darkness falling, Reeves was invited to spend the night. As soon as the outlaws fell asleep, he handcuffed them to their beds without waking them. In the morning he arrested them. He marched them the whole 28 miles back to the camp. For the first three miles the mother followed them, cursing Reeves the whole time.

13   Although Reeves liked to surprise outlaws, he couldn't always do that. So he sometimes squared off against them face-to-face. That was the case when Reeves tracked down Jim Webb. Webb was among the worst outlaws in the Wild West. He was a thief and a killer. He had been on the run two years for shooting a black preacher when Bass Reeves finally cornered him. Although they were 500 yards apart, Webb began firing as fast as he could.

14   Reeves felt bullets whistling past him. One hit his saddle. Another cut a button off his coat. A third cut the reins out of his hands. Reeves didn't flinch. As he leaped off his horse, a fourth shot from Webb ripped through his hat. Still, Reeves stayed calm. He pulled out his rifle and took careful aim. Then he fired twice. Webb fell dead in his tracks.

15   Over Reeves's long career as a marshal, he killed a total of 14 men. But he fired his gun only in self-defense. Once Reeves was arrested for murder. He had shot and killed an outlaw whom he was trying to arrest. But during the trial he proved the outlaw had fired first. The court found him not guilty.

16   Reeves loved the law. One day near the end of his career he showed everyone just how much he loved it. He learned that a new arrest warrant had been issued. It was for a man who had shot and killed his wife. But this time the criminal was not a stranger. It was Reeves's own son.

17   No one expected Reeves to handle the arrest. But he was determined to do his duty. Sadly, he picked up the warrant and went out after his son. Two weeks later, Reeves arrested him. The son was found guilty and was punished with a long jail sentence.

18   In 1907 Bass Reeves turned in his badge. He was ready to retire. That same year, Oklahoma became a state. The days of the old Wild West were gone. Bass Reeves had helped bring law and order to the region. Three years later, at the age of 72, Bass Reeves died.

If you have been timed while reading this article, enter your reading time below. Then turn to the Words-per-Minute Table on page 55 and look up your reading speed (words per minute). Enter your reading speed on the graph on page 56.

Reading Time: Lesson 3

———— : ————
Minutes   *Seconds*

A Finding the Main Idea

One statement below expresses the main idea of the article. One statement is too general, or too broad. The other statement explains only part of the article; it is too narrow. Label the statements using the following key:

M—Main Idea   B—Too Broad   N—Too Narrow

_____ 1. Bass Reeves, one of the best marshals in the Wild West, used disguises and knowledge of the region to capture over 3,000 criminals in 32 years.

_____ 2. Bass Reeves captured more than 3,000 criminals during his years as a U.S. marshal.

_____ 3. Bass Reeves was one of the best marshals in the Wild West.

_____ Score 15 points for a correct M answer.

_____ Score 5 points for each correct B or N answer.

_____ **Total Score:** Finding the Main Idea

B Recalling Facts

How well do you remember the facts in the article? Put an X in the box next to the answer that correctly completes each statement about the article.

1. Bass Reeves started out as
☐ a. an outlaw.
☐ b. a slave.
☐ c. a marshal.

2. Oklahoma was a lawless area in the late 1800s because
☐ a. it was not yet a state.
☐ b. Indians lived in the area.
☐ c. many outlaws hid there.

3. To catch criminals, Reeves often
☐ a. wore a disguise.
☐ b. shot at them.
☐ c. talked to local Indians.

4. Throughout his long career as a marshal, Reeves
☐ a. never killed anyone.
☐ b. only used his gun in self-defense.
☐ c. was arrested for murder several times.

5. Towards the end of Reeves's career,
☐ a. Oklahoma became a state.
☐ b. he turned in his badge.
☐ c. he arrested his own son for murder.

Score 5 points for each correct answer.

_____ **Total Score:** Recalling Facts

C | Making Inferences

When you combine your own experience with information from a text to draw a conclusion that is not directly stated in that text, you are making an inference. Below are five statements that may or may not be inferences based on information in the article. Label the statements using the following key:

C—Correct Inference   **F—Faulty Inference**

_____ 1. Bass Reeves lived with Indians for more than 10 years.

_____ 2. Arkansas became a state before Oklahoma.

_____ 3. Most outlaws did not recognize Reeves's face.

_____ 4. Reeves believed that the law was fair.

_____ 5. After it became a state, Oklahoma no longer needed marshals.

Score 5 points for each correct answer.

_____ **Total Score:** Making Inferences

D | Using Words Precisely

Each numbered sentence below contains an underlined word or phrase from the article. Following the sentence are three definitions. One definition is closest to the meaning of the underlined word. One definition is opposite or nearly opposite. Label those two definitions using the following key; do not label the remaining definition.

C—Closest   **O—Opposite or Nearly Opposite**

1. One day in the early 1860s, he <u>quarreled</u> with his master.

_____ a. argued

_____ b. worked

_____ c. agreed

2. In 1865 slavery was <u>abolished</u>.

_____ a. outlawed

_____ b. ended

_____ c. kept

3. They never even <u>wounded</u> him.

_____ a. healed

_____ b. hurt

_____ c. hit

4. To make it look <u>authentic</u>, Reeves shot three holes in it.

_____ a. real

_____ b. fake

_____ c. old

5. The mother <u>took pity on</u> Reeves.

_____ a. didn't care about

_____ b. laughed at

_____ c. felt sorry for

_____ Score 3 points for each correct C answer.

_____ Score 2 points for each correct O answer.

_____ **Total Score:** Using Words Precisely

Enter the four total scores in the spaces below, and add them together to find your Reading Comprehension Score. Then record your score on the graph on page 57.

Score	Question Type	Lesson 3
_____	Finding the Main Idea	
_____	Recalling Facts	
_____	Making Inferences	
_____	Using Words Precisely	
_____	**Reading Comprehension Score**	

Author's Approach

Put an X in the box next to the correct answer.

1. The main purpose of the first paragraph is to

☐ a. introduce Bass Reeves.

☐ b. describe Oklahoma in the late 1800s.

☐ c. describe law enforcement in the Wild West.

2. Which of the following statements from the article best describes Bass Reeves's reputation as a U.S. marshal?

☐ a. Bass Reeves was one of the best lawmen in the Wild West.

☐ b. [Reeves] knew it was safer to sneak up on outlaws than make a direct charge at them.

☐ c. Bass Reeves had helped bring law and order to the region.

3. What do the authors imply by saying, "No one could have predicted such a future for Reeves"?

☐ a. Bass Reeves did not seem like the type of person who would make a good marshal.

☐ b. It seemed unlikely that someone who was once a slave and an outlaw would become a U.S. marshal.

☐ c. Reeves did not want to be a U.S. marshal.

_____ Number of correct answers

Record your personal assessment of your work on the Critical Thinking Chart on page 58.

Summarizing and Paraphrasing

Follow the directions provided for questions 1 and 2. Put an X in the box next to the correct answer for question 3.

1. Look for the important ideas and events in paragraphs 3 and 4. Summarize those paragraphs in one or two sentences.

_____

_____

_____

_____

2. Reread paragraph 8 in the article. Below, write a summary of the paragraph in no more than 25 words.

_____

_____

_____

_____

Reread your summary and decide whether it covers the important ideas in the paragraph. Next, decide how to shorten the summary to 15 words or less without leaving out any essential information. Write this summary below.

_____

_____

_____

_____

3. Choose the best one-sentence paraphrase for the following sentence from the article: "Like all marshals, Bass Reeves was a marked man."

☐ a. You could tell a marshal just by looking at him.

☐ b. Outlaws wanted to see all marshals, including Reeves, dead.

☐ c. Outlaws often tried to kill marshals.

_____ Number of correct answers

Record your personal assessment of your work on the Critical Thinking Chart on page 58.

Critical Thinking

Put an X in the box next to the correct answer for questions 1 and 5. Follow the directions provided for questions 2, 3, and 4.

1. Which of the following statements from the article is an opinion rather than a fact?

☐ a. No one could have predicted such a future for Reeves.

☐ b. Reeves got the job in part because he knew the region well.

☐ c. As soon as the outlaws fell asleep, he handcuffed them to their beds without waking them.

2. Choose from the letters below to complete the following statement. Write the letters on the lines.

On the positive side, _____, but on the negative side, _____.

a. he fired his gun only in self-defense

b. he had to arrest his own son

c. Bass Reeves captured more than 3,000 criminals as a marshal

3. In which paragraph(s) did you find the information or details to answer question 2? _____

4. Choose from the letters below to correctly complete the following statement. Write the letters on the lines.

   According to paragraph 7, _____ because _____.

   a. Bass Reeves often wore disguises

   b. he knew it was safer to sneak up on outlaws than to make a direct charge at them

   c. he was afraid of the outlaws

5. Into which of the following theme categories would this article fit?

   ☐ a. adventure

   ☐ b. mystery

   ☐ c. western

   _____ Number of correct answers

   Record your personal assessment of your work on the Critical Thinking Chart on page 58.

Personal Response

How do you think you would feel if you were an outlaw and Bass Reeves was chasing you?

_____

_____

_____

_____

Self-Assessment

A word or phrase in the article that I do not understand is _____

_____

_____

_____

_____

Avalanche in British Columbia

The distress call went out at 10:16 A.M. "Mayday! Mayday!" was heard over the radio. "Portal Camp has been wiped out by a snowslide. Require . . . all help possible."

2   One hundred forty men worked and lived at Portal Camp. The camp was part of a copper mine run by the Granduc Mining Company. It was in a remote part of northern British Columbia. Stewart, the nearest town, was 30 miles away.

An avalanche similar to this one destroyed Portal Camp.

3   The mine had been open only six months. It was built under a snow-covered mountain. Portal Camp was near the entrance to the mining tunnel. The camp was like a little town. It had a dining hall, offices, and bunkhouses. The men who lived in the camp took turns working in the mine.

4   In some ways, life wasn't so bad for the miners. They got plenty to eat. They kept each other company. During their free hours they could go to the recreation hall. Still, they were in a place with terrible weather. This part of Canada had fiercely cold winters. It also got huge amounts of snow. Often more than 60 feet fell in a single season. The record snowfall was more than 90 feet.

5   In mid-February 1965, 16 feet of snow fell on the camp. That didn't trouble the miners. To them, the snow just seemed like a nuisance. In truth, however, all that snow posed a great danger.

6   Above Portal Camp sat the Leduc Glacier. This frozen mass of ice lay at the top of the mountain. As new snow piled up on the glacier's smooth surface, the conditions became perfect for an avalanche. It was just a matter of time.

7   On February 18 the time came. Tons of snow slipped down the face of the glacier. There was no warning. The snow came silently, so none of the men had a chance to run away. The lucky miners were the ones in the tunnel. The unlucky ones were at Portal Camp. There the snow blasted all but one building.

8   Gus Ritchie was one of about 100 men in the mine when the avalanche hit. "The slide cut off the power," he said. "We groped our way through the darkness until we got near the entrance." There they found a pile of snow blocking their way. "We crawled up over the snow and were amazed by what we saw. [There was] no more mechanic shop, no more garage, no more coffee shop. Everything was just chunks of wood, steel, and tin."

9   Was anyone alive under all that rubble? It didn't seem possible. Then Ritchie heard a faint moan. He and the others started digging as fast as they could for the survivor. They heard another groan a few feet away. They thought they were digging in the wrong place, so they moved to the new spot. Then they heard several more human sounds. "We were all confused," said Ritchie. "There were people buried all over the place." They dug out eight comrades who were hurt but alive.

10   They also found a dead miner. "It really hurt me when I found my friend Scotty dead," said Ritchie. "He was in a crouched position on his hands and knees. [He] must have died that way as he tried to protect himself from the slide."

11   One survivor at the camp was Frank Sutherland. He was in the kitchen when the snow struck. "First thing I knew, the lights went out." he said. "Then the building took off down the slope and slid half a mile. They had to cut me out with a chain saw"

12   Bertram Owen-Jones, a cook, was also in the kitchen. He was holding a knife when everything went black. The snow blew apart the cookhouse. A piece of the wall fell on Owen-Jones. Still, he never let go of the knife. It took him three hours, but he used the knife to cut himself free. Other men also managed to free themselves.

13 Meanwhile, rescuers were struggling to reach Portal Camp. These rescuers came from both Canada and the United States. They couldn't drive trucks into the mining camp. The 16 feet of new snow blocked all the roads. Some took Snow Cats over the mountains. Others came by air.

14 After several hours, rescuers finally reached the camp. They picked up 17 miners who were in the worst shape and rushed them to safety. But that left more than 120 men still in the camp. Another avalanche could begin at any moment. The rescuers knew they would have to make more trips to Portal Camp to save these men.

15 By the next day, though, they found it almost impossible to get to the camp. A blizzard was raging there. Wind whipped the snow in all directions. No one could see more than a few yards. Still, helicopter pilots bravely agreed to fly into the camp. One of these pilots was Kenny Eichner. He wanted to bring in a doctor to treat wounded miners stranded at the camp.

16 About a mile from Portal Camp, the storm became too intense. Eichner had to land his chopper right on top of the glacier. All night he and the doctor huddled inside the helicopter. The next morning Eichner had to chip ice off the blades to get going again.

17 Even after reaching the camp, rescuers were not safe. The threat of another avalanche hung over them all the time. Some filled their choppers with surviving miners and flew out again. Others stayed to look for men still trapped in the snow. Hour after hour they dug. They found one dead body after another. In time their hopes of finding survivors faded.

18 After 79 hours they found a buried miner who was still alive. He had been trapped under six feet of snow. Helicopters had landed on top of him. At last a bulldozer began to clear away the snow above him. That was when rescuers found him. He was dehydrated. He had frostbite. But at least he was alive.

19 After a week of hard work, rescuers still had not sifted through all the snow. But they could stay no longer. So much new snow was falling that another avalanche seemed sure to come. Everyone had to get out of Portal Camp. So now the rescuers themselves had to be rescued.

20 More pilots flew in through the blinding blizzard. These men spotted Portal Camp only because smoke was still rising from the ruins. The storm was so bad that one plane slid off the runway at Stewart and hit a snowbank.

21 In all, 26 miners died. More would have died if it hadn't been for the skill and courage of the rescuers. Portal Camp was never reopened. The risk of more avalanches was just too great. The Granduc Mining Company had learned a harsh lesson. There are some places that should be disturbed only by Nature.

If you have been timed while reading this article, enter your reading time below. Then turn to the Words-per-Minute Table on page 55 and look up your reading speed (words per minute). Enter your reading speed on the graph on page 56.

Reading Time: Lesson 4

———— : ————
Minutes   Seconds

A | Finding the Main Idea

One statement below expresses the main idea of the article. One statement is too general, or too broad. The other statement explains only part of the article; it is too narrow. Label the statements using the following key:

M—Main Idea   **B—Too Broad**   **N—Too Narrow**

_____ 1. An avalanche covered the Portal Camp mining camp in British Columbia in February 1965.

_____ 2. A dangerous avalanche in the remote Portal Camp mining camp prompted a dangerous rescue mission and showed that there are some parts of nature that should be left alone.

_____ 3. Sixteen feet of snow fell on the Portal Camp mining camp in February 1965.

_____ Score 15 points for a correct M answer.

_____ Score 5 points for each correct B or N answer.

_____ **Total Score:** Finding the Main Idea

B | Recalling Facts

How well do you remember the facts in the article? Put an X in the box next to the answer that correctly completes each statement about the article.

1. Portal Camp was
   - ☐ a. in Stewart, British Columbia.
   - ☐ b. part of a gold mine run by the Granduc Mining Company.
   - ☐ c. built under a snow-covered mountain.

2. The part of Canada that Portal Camp was in
   - ☐ a. often got more than 60 feet of snow in one season.
   - ☐ b. got an average of 16 feet of snow during the winter.
   - ☐ c. usually had mild winters.

3. The avalanche was most dangerous for the
   - ☐ a. rescuers trying to enter the camp.
   - ☐ b. workers in the mines.
   - ☐ c. miners at Portal Camp.

4. Rescuers had to enter Portal Camp
   - ☐ a. in large trucks.
   - ☐ b. by helicopter.
   - ☐ c. by climbing over the mountains on foot.

5. Rescuers stopped looking for survivors after a week because
   - ☐ a. it seemed likely that there would be another avalanche.
   - ☐ b. they had found all the miners.
   - ☐ c. there was a blizzard in the area.

Score 5 points for each correct answer.

_____ **Total Score:** Recalling Facts

C Making Inferences

When you combine your own experience with information from a text to draw a conclusion that is not directly stated in that text, you are making an inference. Below are five statements that may or may not be inferences based on information in the article. Label the statements using the following key:

C—Correct Inference   **F—Faulty Inference**

_____ 1. Miners usually lived away from their homes most of the year.

_____ 2. The Granduc Mining Company did not know about the Leduc Glacier when it set up Portal Camp.

_____ 3. The miners were not aware of the possibility of an avalanche.

_____ 4. The miners at Portal Camp liked snow.

_____ 5. It is possible to survive being buried under a snowbank for more than three days.

Score 5 points for each correct answer.

_____ **Total Score:** Making Inferences

D Using Words Precisely

Each numbered sentence below contains an underlined word or phrase from the article. Following the sentence are three definitions. One definition is closest to the meaning of the underlined word. One definition is opposite or nearly opposite. Label those two definitions using the following key; do not label the remaining definition.

C—Closest   **O—Opposite or Nearly Opposite**

1. To them, the snow just seemed like a <u>nuisance</u>.

_____ a. burden

_____ b. help

_____ c. bother

2. Then Ritchie heard a <u>faint</u> moan.

_____ a. quiet

_____ b. far away

_____ c. loud

3. They dug out eight <u>comrades</u> who were hurt but alive.

_____ a. enemies

_____ b. people

_____ c. co-workers

4. About a mile from Portal Camp, the storm became too <u>intense</u>.

_____ a. fast

_____ b. strong

_____ c. mild

5. In time their hopes of finding survivors <u>faded</u>.

_____ a. held strong

_____ b. grew

_____ c. dimmed

_____ Score 3 points for each correct C answer.

_____ Score 2 points for each correct O answer.

_____ **Total Score:** Using Words Precisely

Enter the four total scores in the spaces below, and add them together to find your Reading Comprehension Score. Then record your score on the graph on page 57.

Score	Question Type	Lesson 4
_____	Finding the Main Idea	
_____	Recalling Facts	
_____	Making Inferences	
_____	Using Words Precisely	
_____	**Reading Comprehension Score**	

Author's Approach

Put an X in the box next to the correct answer.

1. The authors use the first sentence of the article to

☐ a. get the reader's attention.

☐ b. inform the reader about the avalanche.

☐ c. entertain the reader.

2. What is the authors' purpose in writing "Avalanche in British Columbia"?

☐ a. to warn the reader about the dangers of avalanches

☐ b. to describe Portal Camp

☐ c. to inform the reader about the avalanche at Portal Camp

3. Based on the statement from the article, "To [the miners], the snow just seemed like a nuisance," you can conclude that the authors want the reader to think that the miners did not

☐ a. realize that the snow could cause an avalanche.

☐ b. mind the snow.

☐ c. realize how much snow was on the ground.

_____ Number of correct answers

Record your personal assessment of your work on the Critical Thinking Chart on page 58.

Summarizing and Paraphrasing

Follow the directions provided for the questions below.

1. Reread paragraph 8 in the article. Below, write a summary of the paragraph in no more than 25 words.

_____

_____

_____

_____

Reread your summary and decide whether it covers the important ideas in the paragraph. Next, decide how to shorten the summary to 15 words or less without leaving out any essential information. Write this summary below.

_____

_____

_____

_____

2. Complete the following one-sentence summary of the article using the lettered phrases from the phrase bank below. Write the letters on the lines.

Phrase Bank

a. what happened during the avalanche
b. a description of the camp
c. a description of the rescue efforts

The article about the Portal Camp avalanche begins with _____,

goes on to explain _____, and ends with _____.

3. Read the statement from the article below. Then read the paraphrase of that statement. Choose the reason that best tells why the paraphrase does not say the same thing as the statement.

Statement: They dug out eight comrades who were hurt but alive.

Paraphrase: They saved eight of their friends.

☐ a. Paraphrase says too much.

☐ b. Paraphrase doesn't say enough.

☐ c. Paraphrase doesn't agree with the statement from the article.

_____ Number of correct answers

Record your personal assessment of your work on the Critical Thinking Chart on page 58.

Critical Thinking

Put an X in the box next to the correct answer for questions 1, 4, and 5. Follow the directions provided for questions 2 and 3.

1. Which of the following statements from the article is an opinion rather than a fact?

☐ a. As new snow piled up on the glacier's smooth surface, the conditions became perfect for an avalanche.

☐ b. "[He] must have died that way as he tried to protect himself from the slide."

☐ c. Eichner had to land his chopper right on top of the glacier.

2. Choose from the letters below to correctly complete the following statement. Write the letters on the lines.

   According to the article, an avalanche caused _____ to _____, and the effect was that _____.

   a. be destroyed

   b. many miners were killed or injured

   c. Portal Camp

3. Which paragraphs provide evidence from the article to support your answer to question 2? _____

4. Based on Kenny Eichner's actions in the article, you can conclude that he

   ☐ a. cared about the miners.

   ☐ b. never reached the camp.

   ☐ c. did not want to pilot a helicopter again after leaving Portal Camp.

5. Into which of the following theme categories would this story fit?

   ☐ a. mystery

   ☐ b. adventure

   ☐ c. historical anecdote

   ┌───┐
   │ _____ Number of correct answers   │
   │   │
   │ Record your personal assessment of your work on the │
   │ Critical Thinking Chart on page 58.   │
   └───┘

Personal Response

I know how the miners felt when the avalanche began coming down because _____

_____

_____

_____

_____

Self-Assessment

When reading the article, I was having trouble with _____

_____

_____

_____

_____

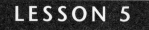

The Spy Who Saved Lincoln

Abraham Lincoln is sworn in for his second term as president in 1865.

"But why—why do they want to kill me?" asked Abraham Lincoln.

2   It was February 21, 1861. Allan Pinkerton, head of the Pinkerton National Detective Agency, tried to explain. He pointed out that many people in the South hated Lincoln. They hated him with a passion. To them, he was a symbol of the end of slavery and the Southern way of life. Some of these people wanted to see Lincoln dead. A few were even willing to give up their own lives to kill him.

3   Lincoln had been elected president of the United States in 1860. But he had not yet taken the oath of office. That would happen on March 4, 1861. If some Southerners had their way, Lincoln would not live to be president. It was Pinkerton's job to see that these angry Southerners did not kill the future president.

4   Pinkerton knew of the dangers Lincoln faced because he had sent some of his spies to Baltimore, Maryland. The spies posed as Lincoln-haters. They went to secret meetings. These meetings were held to see what could be done about Lincoln. It was at these meetings that Pinkerton's spies learned just how strong Southern anger really was.

5   One man felt an especially powerful rage. He was a barber named Cypriano Ferrandini. At one of the secret meetings, he called the future president "most vile and repulsive." The crowd roared in agreement. They raised clenched fists. Next Ferrandini took out a knife and waved it over his head. He shouted, "Lincoln shall never, never be president. My life is of no consequence in a cause like this. I am willing to give it for his."

6   When Pinkerton's spies reported back to him, Pinkerton could barely believe them. Were the Southerners serious? Or were the wild speeches nothing but hot air? Pinkerton felt he had to check it out for himself. So he went to Baltimore. Like his spies, he pretended to hate Lincoln. Before long, he was introduced to Ferrandini. The two men began to talk. Pinkerton asked the barber if there was any way to save the South without killing Lincoln. "No," said Ferrandini. "He must die—and die he shall." That convinced Pinkerton that the men *were* serious. They wouldn't blink at killing a man they saw as their enemy.

7   Lincoln listened closely to Pinkerton's report. Still, he was not sure the threat was real. But the very next day, he heard the same story from Frederick Seward, a trusted friend. It didn't seem likely that both Seward and Pinkerton were wrong. So he turned to Allan Pinkerton. "What do you want me to do?" he asked.

8   Pinkerton knew Lincoln was about to travel from Pennsylvania to Washington, D.C. On his way, he would pass through Baltimore. Pinkerton feared this was when the killers would strike.

9   Lincoln was supposed to arrive in Baltimore by train on February 23. Then he would make his way to another railroad station on the other side of town. He would ride a carriage through the streets. That would give people a chance to come out and wave to him. But it would also give an assassin the perfect chance to attack. In fact, Pinkerton knew, the killers might strike anywhere along the route to Washington. They might blow up a

bridge as Lincoln's train crossed it. Or they could attack Lincoln with guns while he was riding in his carriage. Or a single man could sneak up on him with a knife at the train station. Lincoln couldn't count on the police to save him. The head of Baltimore's police force was himself a Lincoln-hater.

10 Pinkerton thought of all the options. Then he decided Lincoln should play it safe. He advised him to change his schedule, but keep the change a secret. He said Lincoln should leave for Washington right away instead of waiting until the next morning. That way he would be in and out of Baltimore before Ferrandini's men ever knew about it.

11 Lincoln refused to do this. He had promised to attend two important events before leaving Pennsylvania. "Whatever the cost, these two promises I must fulfill," he told Pinkerton.

12 So Pinkerton tried again. Why not leave just 12 hours early? That way Lincoln could keep his promises, but still change his schedule enough to evade the killers. Lincoln agreed. Instead of leaving for Washington on the 23rd, he would leave late at night on the 22nd.

13 Secrecy was vital. Only a few people knew of the change in plans. To be extra safe, Pinkerton had the telegraph lines cut. That way if anyone did find out about the change of plans, they couldn't warn the assassins.

14 To be sure no one noticed him, Lincoln traveled in a kind of disguise. He didn't wear his famous stovepipe hat. He wore a soft felt hat. He also tossed an overcoat loosely over his shoulders.

15 Just before midnight, Lincoln boarded a special train in Harrisburg, Pennsylvania. It would take him to Philadelphia. There a second train waited. This second train would whisk Lincoln straight to Washington, D.C. It would pass through Baltimore, but he would not have to get out.

16 Still, there might be danger. Pinkerton feared the assassins would somehow learn of the change in plans. Then they could plant a bomb under one of the railroad bridges. They could kill Lincoln by blowing up the whole train.

17 These doubts troubled Pinkerton. He wouldn't rest easy until the president was safely in Washington. So all night Pinkerton stood on the rear platform of Lincoln's special train. He had spies stationed all along the route. If there was any sign of trouble, they would signal Pinkerton. He would then immediately stop the train. Fortunately, there was no problem. The train arrived early the next morning in Washington.

18 There was one final scare, however. As Lincoln stepped off the train, a man shouted out to him. "Abe," he yelled, "you can't play that one on me." Pinkerton thought the stranger might be an assassin. He moved to attack him.

19 "Don't strike him!" yelled Lincoln. It turned out the stranger was a friend of Lincoln's who had recognized him despite the disguise.

20 After people heard about the plot to kill Lincoln, the assassins went into hiding. They did not kill him. And they did not keep him from becoming president. Still, most Southerners refused to accept him as their leader. One after another, Southern states seceded from the Union. One month after Lincoln took office, the Civil War began.

21 The war lasted four long and bloody years. Then, just a few days after the war ended, John Wilkes Booth did what Ferrandini had failed to do. He shot President Lincoln in the back of the head on April 14, 1865. Allan Pinkerton was in Chicago when it happened. Sadly, he wasn't around to save Abraham Lincoln a second time.

If you have been timed while reading this article, enter your reading time below. Then turn to the Words-per-Minute Table on page 55 and look up your reading speed (words per minute). Enter your reading speed on the graph on page 56.

Reading Time: Lesson 5

———— : ————
Minutes   Seconds

A Finding the Main Idea

One statement below expresses the main idea of the article. One statement is too general, or too broad. The other statement explains only part of the article; it is too narrow. Label the statements using the following key:

M—Main Idea   **B—Too Broad**   **N—Too Narrow**

_____ 1. When he learned that Abraham Lincoln's life was in danger, detective Allan Pinkerton devised a plan to keep the future president safe.

_____ 2. Southerner Cypriano Ferrandini wanted to kill Abraham Lincoln when he traveled through Baltimore.

_____ 3. Allan Pinkerton helped Abraham Lincoln arrive safely in Washington, D.C.

_____ Score 15 points for a correct M answer.

_____ Score 5 points for each correct B or N answer.

_____ **Total Score:** Finding the Main Idea

B Recalling Facts

How well do you remember the facts in the article? Put an X in the box next to the answer that correctly completes each statement about the article.

1. Many Southerners wanted Abraham Lincoln dead because
   - ☐ a. he had not yet taken the oath of office.
   - ☐ b. they feared he would end slavery and their way of life.
   - ☐ c. they wanted to kill him.

2. Pinkerton first learned of the danger to Lincoln
   - ☐ a. through spies posing as Lincoln-haters.
   - ☐ b. by talking to Cypriano Ferrandini.
   - ☐ c. from Lincoln's friend Frederick Seward.

3. To be safe, Pinkerton advised Lincoln to
   - ☐ a. avoid going through Baltimore.
   - ☐ b. cancel his trip to Washington, D.C.
   - ☐ c. change his schedule by leaving 12 hours earlier.

4. After Lincoln arrived safely in Washington, D.C., the
   - ☐ a. assassins went into hiding.
   - ☐ b. assassins gave up their plans to kill Lincoln.
   - ☐ c. South accepted him as their leader.

5. After the Civil War ended,
   - ☐ a. Pinkerton saved Lincoln's life again in Chicago.
   - ☐ b. Ferrandini plotted to kill Lincoln again.
   - ☐ c. John Wilkes Booth shot President Lincoln.

Score 5 points for each correct answer.

_____ **Total Score:** Recalling Facts

C | Making Inferences

When you combine your own experience with information from a text to draw a conclusion that is not directly stated in that text, you are making an inference. Below are five statements that may or may not be inferences based on information in the article. Label the statements using the following key:

C—Correct Inference   **F—Faulty Inference**

_____ 1. In 1861 Southerners were not able to vote for the president.

_____ 2. Southerners were afraid of what Lincoln would do if he were president.

_____ 3. Baltimore was the center of the movement against Lincoln.

_____ 4. Lincoln was known for wearing a stovepipe hat.

_____ 5. Allan Pinkerton had a lot of experience protecting presidents.

Score 5 points for each correct answer.

_____ **Total Score:** Making Inferences

D | Using Words Precisely

Each numbered sentence below contains an underlined word or phrase from the article. Following the sentence are three definitions. One definition is closest to the meaning of the underlined word. One definition is opposite or nearly opposite. Label those two definitions using the following key; do not label the remaining definition.

C—Closest   **O—Opposite or Nearly Opposite**

1. They hated him with a <u>passion</u>.

_____ a. a lack of caring

_____ b. interest

_____ c. strong feeling

2. One man felt an especially powerful <u>rage</u>.

_____ a. anger

_____ b. calm

_____ c. emotion

3. They raised <u>clenched</u> fists.

_____ a. strong

_____ b. open

_____ c. closed

4. Secrecy was <u>vital</u>.

_____ a. necessary

_____ b. kept

_____ c. unimportant

5. This second train would <u>whisk</u> Lincoln straight to Washington, D.C.

_____ a. slowly take

_____ b. carry

_____ c. rush

_____ Score 3 points for each correct C answer.

_____ Score 2 points for each correct O answer.

_____ **Total Score:** Using Words Precisely

Enter the four total scores in the spaces below, and add them together to find your Reading Comprehension Score. Then record your score on the graph on page 57.

Score	Question Type	Lesson 5
_____	Finding the Main Idea	
_____	Recalling Facts	
_____	Making Inferences	
_____	Using Words Precisely	
_____	**Reading Comprehension Score**	

Author's Approach

Put an X in the box next to the correct answer.

1. The main purpose of the second paragraph is to

☐ a. introduce Allan Pinkerton.

☐ b. give background information for the story.

☐ c. describe Abraham Lincoln.

2. What is the authors' purpose in writing "The Spy Who Saved Lincoln"?

☐ a. to describe the work of Pinkerton's detective agency

☐ b. to convey the mood of the South in 1861

☐ c. to inform the reader about how Pinkerton saved Lincoln from being killed

3. Which of the following statements from the article best describes Southerners' feelings about Lincoln?

☐ a. To them, he meant the end of slavery and the Southern way of life.

☐ b. At one of the secret meetings, [Ferrandini] called the future president "most vile and repulsive."

☐ c. They wouldn't blink at killing a man they saw as their enemy.

_____ Number of correct answers

Record your personal assessment of your work on the Critical Thinking Chart on page 58.

Summarizing and Paraphrasing

Follow the directions provided for question 1. Put an X in the box next to the correct answer for question 2.

1. Look for the important ideas and events in paragraphs 5 and 6. Summarize those paragraphs in one or two sentences.

_____

_____

_____

_____

2. Read the statement from the article below. Then read the paraphrase of that statement. Choose the reason that best tells why the paraphrase does not say the same thing as the statement.

   Statement: It was at these meetings that Pinkerton's spies learned just how strong Southern anger really was.

   Paraphrase: At these meetings Pinkerton's spies learned that Southerners did not like Lincoln.

   ☐ a. Paraphrase says too much.

   ☐ b. Paraphrase doesn't say enough.

   ☐ c. Paraphrase doesn't agree with the statement from the article.

   _____ Number of correct answers

   Record your personal assessment of your work on the Critical Thinking Chart on page 58.

Critical Thinking

Follow the directions provided for questions 1, 3, 4, and 5. Put an X in the box next to the correct answer for question 2.

1. For each statement below, write O if it expresses an opinion or F if it expresses a fact.

   _____ a. It was Pinkerton's job to see that these angry Southerners did not kill the future president.

   _____ b. "Lincoln shall never, never be president."

   _____ c. Pinkerton thought the stranger might be an assassin.

2. From the information in the article, you can conclude that

   ☐ a. Southerners were still angry at Lincoln after the Civil War.

   ☐ b. there were several attempts to assassinate Lincoln.

   ☐ c. Pinkerton was no longer doing detective work in 1865.

3. Using what you know about the two assassination attempts against Lincoln, list at least two ways in which they were similar and two ways in which they were different.

   Similarities

   _____

   _____

   _____

   Differences

   _____

   _____

   _____

CRITICAL THINKING

4. In which paragraph(s) did you find the information to support your answers to question 3? _____

5. Choose from the letters below to correctly complete the following statement. Write the letters on the lines.

   According to paragraph 17, _____ because _____.

   a. he needed to watch for signals from his spies

   b. the train arrived safely in Washington

   c. Pinkerton stood on the back of Lincoln's train

   _____ Number of correct answers

   Record your personal assessment of your work on the Critical Thinking Chart on page 58.

Personal Response

What was most surprising or interesting to you about this article?

_____

_____

_____

_____

Self-Assessment

From reading this article, I have learned _____

_____

_____

_____

_____

Compare and Contrast

Think about the articles you have read in Unit One. Pick the three articles you thought described the most interesting jobs. Write the titles of the articles in the first column of the chart below. Use information you have learned from the articles to fill in the empty boxes in the chart.

Title	What job does the central person or people in this article have?	What difficult situation did the person or people in this article encounter?	Do you think people with this job encounter difficult situations often? Why or why not?

Which line of work that you read about interested you most? _____ Why? _____

_____

_____

Words-per-Minute Table

Unit One

Directions: If you were timed while reading an article, refer to the Reading Time you recorded in the box at the end of the article. Use this Words-per-Minute Table to determine your reading speed for that article. Then plot your reading speed on the graph on page 56.

Lesson	Sample	1	2	3	4	5	
No. of Words	809	1,076	891	1,126	1,147	1,147	
1:30	539	717	594	751	765	765	**90**
1:40	485	646	535	676	688	688	**100**
1:50	441	587	486	614	626	626	**110**
2:00	405	538	446	563	574	574	**120**
2:10	373	497	411	520	529	529	**130**
2:20	347	461	382	483	492	492	**140**
2:30	324	430	356	450	459	459	**150**
2:40	303	404	334	422	430	430	**160**
2:50	286	380	314	397	405	405	**170**
3:00	270	359	297	375	382	382	**180**
3:10	255	340	281	356	362	362	**190**
3:20	243	323	267	338	344	344	**200**
3:30	231	307	255	322	328	328	**210**
3:40	221	293	243	307	313	313	**220**
3:50	211	281	232	294	299	299	**230**
4:00	202	269	223	282	287	287	**240**
4:10	194	258	214	270	275	275	**250**
4:20	187	248	206	260	265	265	**260**
4:30	180	239	198	250	255	255	**270**
4:40	173	231	191	241	246	246	**280**
4:50	167	223	184	233	237	237	**290**
5:00	162	215	178	225	229	229	**300**
5:10	157	208	172	218	222	222	**310**
5:20	152	202	167	211	215	215	**320**
5:30	147	196	162	751	209	209	**330**
5:40	143	190	157	199	202	202	**340**
5:50	139	184	153	193	197	197	**350**
6:00	135	179	149	188	191	191	**360**
6:10	131	174	144	183	186	186	**370**
6:20	128	170	141	676	181	181	**380**
6:30	124	166	137	173	176	176	**390**
6:40	121	161	134	169	172	172	**400**
6:50	118	157	130	165	168	168	**410**
7:00	116	154	127	161	164	164	**420**
7:10	113	150	124	157	160	160	**430**
7:20	110	147	122	154	156	156	**440**
7:30	108	143	119	150	153	153	**450**
7:40	106	140	116	147	150	150	**460**
7:50	103	137	114	144	146	146	**470**
8:00	101	135	111	141	143	143	**480**

Minutes and Seconds

Seconds

Plotting Your Progress: Reading Speed

Unit One

Directions: If you were timed while reading an article, write your words-per-minute rate for that article in the box under the number of the lesson. Then plot your reading speed on the graph by putting a small X on the line directly above the number of the lesson, across from the number of words per minute you read. As you mark your speed for each lesson, graph your progress by drawing a line to connect the X's.

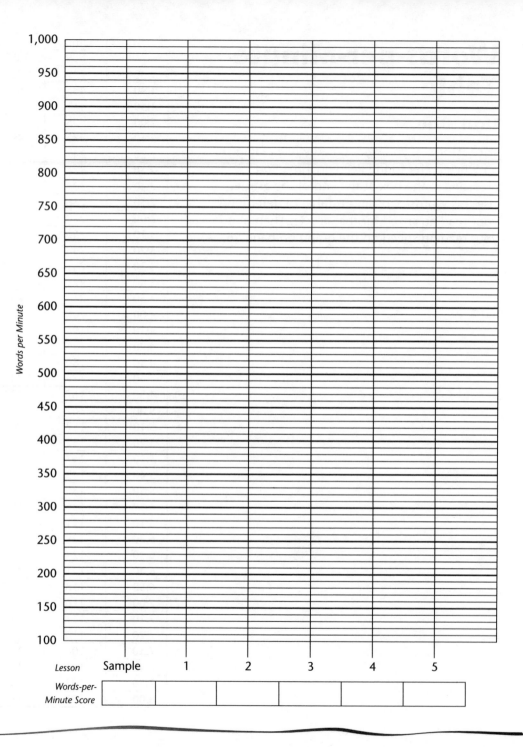

Plotting Your Progress: Reading Comprehension

Unit One

Directions: Write your Reading Comprehension score for each lesson in the box under the number of the lesson. Then plot your score on the graph by putting a small X on the line directly above the number of the lesson and across from the score you earned. As you mark your score for each lesson, graph your progress by drawing a line to connect the X's.

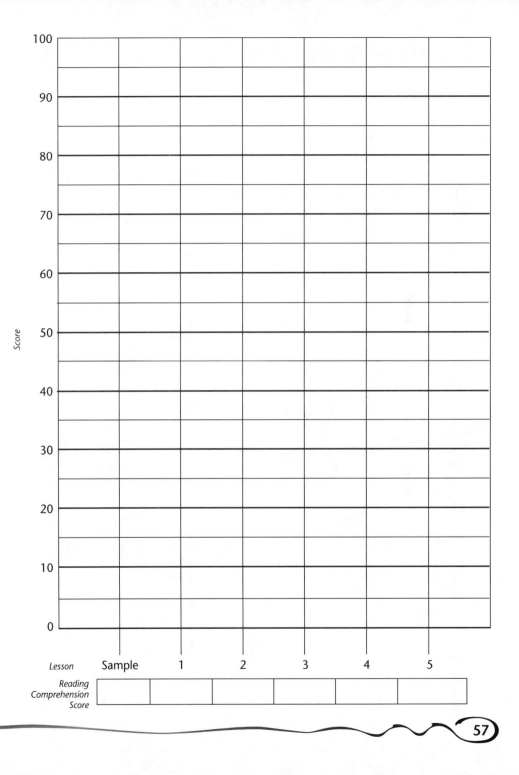

Lesson	Sample	1	2	3	4	5
Reading Comprehension Score						

Plotting Your Progress: Critical Thinking

Unit One

Directions: Work with your teacher to evaluate your responses to the Critical Thinking questions for each lesson. Then fill in the appropriate spaces in the chart below. For each lesson and each type of Critical Thinking question, do the following: Mark a minus sign (–) in the box to indicate areas in which you feel you could improve. Mark a plus sign (+) to indicate areas in which you feel you did well. Mark a minus-slash-plus sign (–/+) to indicate areas in which you had mixed success. Then write any comments you have about your performance, including ideas for improvement.

Lesson	Author's Approach	Summarizing and Paraphrasing	Critical Thinking
Sample			
1			
2			
3			
4			
5			

UNIT TWO

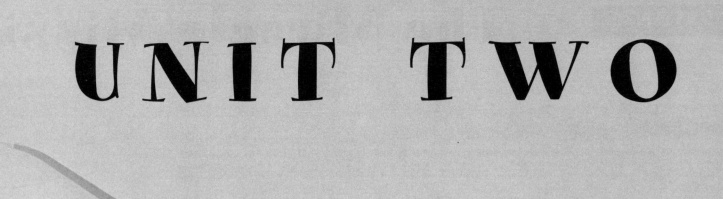

The Miracle Mission

The B-17 bomber was like a turtle—slow and steady. It was meant to fly in a straight line to its target, drop its bombs, and fly in a straight line back home. The B-17 bomber had little ability to dodge enemy planes. And it surely couldn't outrace them. Yet this famed World War II plane had one major thing going for it. It was hard to shoot down. B-17s often returned to their bases shot full of holes or with a chunk of a wing or tail missing. The four-engine plane could sputter home even with one or two engines knocked out.

2 Lieutenant Edward Michael flew one of these tough B-17s. He named it

The B-17 bomber was not very fast, but it was hard to shoot down.

Bertie Lee after his wife. On one bombing mission, the *Bertie Lee* came back with 144 holes in her. Then, on April 11, 1944, the plane endured its greatest test. So, too, did Lieutenant Michael.

3 That morning, he and his crew took off from England. The *Bertie Lee* was part of a 100-plane bombing run over Germany. Around 11 o'clock the planes arrived at their target. Shells from enemy guns on the ground began to burst all around them. They had no sure way to avoid this "flak." B-17 pilots just had to fly through it and hope they were not hit. That wasn't the only danger. German planes began to attack the bombers. Machine gunners on board the B-17s fired back.

4 The best defense the bombers had was to stick together. If they stayed in formation, they could protect each other. But that wasn't always possible. If a B-17 got hit, it might lose power and be unable to keep up. That's what happened to the *Bertie Lee*. Enemy fire riddled the plane with holes from its nose to its tail. The plane lost altitude. It fell out of formation. The *Bertie Lee* was now on its own. The lumbering bomber was like a duck in a shooting gallery.

5 Sensing an easy score, German pilots moved in to finish off the plane. One of their shells blew up the *Bertie Lee's* cockpit. The explosion wounded copilot Franklin Westberg. It injured Edward Michael too. A piece of shrapnel cut deep into his right thigh. The blast blew out a side window and wiped out most of the instruments. Hydraulic fluid splattered the windshield, making it hard to see. Black smoke filled the cockpit, obscuring vision even more. But this was just the beginning. Things were about to get much worse.

6 Michael got a frantic call from the men stationed back in the bomb bay. This was the section of the B-17 where the bombs were stored. The men reported that the bomb bay was on fire. Three shells had hit it, setting it ablaze. The bomb bay was still loaded with 100-pound bombs. These would burn fiercely if the fire reached them. Also, the plane's gas tanks were nearby. If the fire reached the tanks, the entire plane would explode.

7 Michael ordered his crew to drop all the bombs. But the release lever was jammed. The men couldn't get the bombs out.

8   Even though Michael was still over enemy land, he ordered everyone else in the plane to bail out. He thought it was their best chance of staying alive. Seven of his men parachuted. (They all survived, were captured by Germans, and became prisoners of war.) But two men refused to leave him. They were his copilot, Franklin Westberg, and bombardier John Lieber.

9   Lieber grabbed a machine gun and began firing at German planes. Michael saw Lieber and told him to jump. But Leiber's parachute was full of bullet holes. That made it useless. So Michael offered Leiber his own parachute.

10   "No, Mike," replied Leiber. "If we can't go out together, we'll go down together." Westberg also refused to jump. Each man acted out of his sense of duty toward the other two. So, with three men and only two parachutes, they all agreed to stay with the *Bertie Lee*.

11   Michael's instrument panel had been destroyed by German shells, so he was now flying "blind." He had no way of knowing his exact position. He just pointed his plane northwest toward England and hoped the *Bertie Lee* made it there.

12   Meanwhile, Lieber walked through the plane putting out flames. More flak rocked the B-17. Michael took the plane down very close to the ground to avoid it. That seemed to work. But soon enemy soldiers on the ground opened fire on the plane with their rifles.

13   Michael brought the plane up again. But when he reached an altitude of 2,500 feet, enemy fighters were waiting for him. He had to maneuver the plane to evade German fire from the ground *and* from the air. At times, he dropped the plane so low it clipped the tops of trees. Up and down Michael flew, using every trick he knew. Once he even flew straight into a bank of clouds to lose a German fighter plane that was closing in on him.

14   At last, the *Bertie Lee* made it to the North Sea. A short time later, Michael saw the English coast. They were out of enemy territory! Once again, Michael instructed Lieber and Westberg to take the two good parachutes and jump to safety. But again, they refused to leave him. They were in this together and they would take their chances—with him—on a crash landing.

15   By this time, Lieutenant Michael was feeling very weak. The gash in his thigh had caused him to lose a lot of blood. Finally he lost consciousness and Westberg had to take over the controls. Just as the plane approached the landing field, Michael regained consciousness. He had enough strength left to try the landing himself.

16   It had to be a crash landing. The bomb bay doors were stuck open. The wing flaps didn't work. The wheels were useless without a hydraulic system. Yet despite the odds, Michael managed to make a perfect belly landing. The *Bertie Lee* and its three-man crew had made it. Soldiers at the base called it "The Miracle Mission." None of them could believe that a plane so badly shot up could still fly and land safely.

17   It took Lieutenant Edward Michael months to recover. Then, on January 10, 1945, he visited the White House. There he received the Medal of Honor— the nation's highest award. President Franklin D. Roosevelt shook his hand. It was quite an honor. But Michael had one regret. He wished John Lieber and Franklin Westberg had been given medals too. He knew in his heart that they deserved medals just as much as he did.

If you have been timed while reading this article, enter your reading time below. Then turn to the Words-per-Minute Table on page 101 and look up your reading speed (words per minute). Enter your reading speed on the graph on page 102.

Reading Time: Lesson 6

———— : ————
Minutes   Seconds

A │ Finding the Main Idea

One statement below expresses the main idea of the article. One statement is too general, or too broad. The other statement explains only part of the article; it is too narrow. Label the statements using the following key:

M—Main Idea   **B—Too Broad**   **N—Too Narrow**

_____ 1. A piece of shrapnel cut into Lieutenant Edward Michael's thigh when his plane was hit.

_____ 2. Lieutenant Edward Michael piloted a B-17 during World War II.

_____ 3. Lieutenant Edward Michael managed to fly his B-17 from Germany to England even though it had been badly damaged.

_____ Score 15 points for a correct M answer.

_____ Score 5 points for each correct B or N answer.

_____ **Total Score:** Finding the Main Idea

B │ Recalling Facts

How well do you remember the facts in the article? Put an X in the box next to the answer that correctly completes each statement about the article.

1. The B-17 bomber was designed to
   □ a. outrun enemy planes.
   □ b. fly in a group.
   □ c. fly in a straight line and drop bombs.

2. The B-17s tried to fly in formation because that way they
   □ a. could protect each other.
   □ b. could avoid enemy guns.
   □ c. wouldn't lose altitude.

3. When the *Bertie Lee* was hit,
   □ a. one of the engines caught on fire.
   □ b. most of the cockpit instruments were wiped out.
   □ c. Lieutenant Michael was not hurt.

4. Lieutenant Michael tried to fly close to the ground because
   □ a. enemy soldiers on the ground were shooting at him.
   □ b. he didn't know his exact position.
   □ c. he wanted to avoid enemy fighters.

5. Because of his courageous flight, Lieutenant Michael
   □ a. received the Medal of Honor from the President.
   □ b. never flew a B-17 again.
   □ c. took months to recover.

Score 5 points for each correct answer.

_____ **Total Score:** Recalling Facts

C | Making Inferences

When you combine your own experience with information from a text to draw a conclusion that is not directly stated in that text, you are making an inference. Below are five statements that may or may not be inferences based on information in the article. Label the statements using the following key:

C—Correct Inference   **F—Faulty Inference**

_____ 1. B-17s were very valuable during World War II.

_____ 2. B-17s are still used by the army today.

_____ 3. The Germans did not use B-17s during World War II.

_____ 4. John Lieber managed to put out the fires on the *Bertie Lee*.

_____ 5. It is not possible to land a plane if its wing flaps are not working.

Score 5 points for each correct answer.

_____ **Total Score:** Making Inferences

D | Using Words Precisely

Each numbered sentence below contains an underlined word or phrase from the article. Following the sentence are three definitions. One definition is closest to the meaning of the underlined word. One definition is opposite or nearly opposite. Label those two definitions using the following key; do not label the remaining definition.

C—Closest   **O—Opposite or Nearly Opposite**

1. If they stayed <u>in formation</u>, they could protect each other.

_____ a. separated

_____ b. near each other

_____ c. in a special order

2. The <u>lumbering</u> bomber was like a duck in a shooting gallery.

_____ a. clumsy

_____ b. graceful

_____ c. slow

3. Black smoke filled the cockpit, <u>obscuring</u> vision even more.

_____ a. helping

_____ b. clearing

_____ c. blocking

4. Michael got a <u>frantic</u> call from the men stationed back in the bomb bay.

_____ a. panicky

_____ b. calm

_____ c. sudden

5. He had to maneuver the plane to <u>evade</u> German fire from the ground *and* from the air.

_____ a. face

_____ b. go through

_____ c. escape

_____ Score 3 points for each correct C answer.

_____ Score 2 points for each correct O answer.

_____ **Total Score:** Using Words Precisely

Enter the four total scores in the spaces below, and add them together to find your Reading Comprehension Score. Then record your score on the graph on page 103.

Score	Question Type	Lesson 6
_____	Finding the Main Idea	
_____	Recalling Facts	
_____	Making Inferences	
_____	Using Words Precisely	
_____	**Reading Comprehension Score**	

Author's Approach

Put an X in the box next to the correct answer.

1. The main purpose of the first paragraph is to

☐ a. introduce Lieutenant Edward Michael.

☐ b. describe the B-17 bomber.

☐ c. compare the B-17 to other airplanes.

2. Which of the following statements from the article best describes the B-17 bomber?

☐ a. The B-17 was like a turtle—slow and steady.

☐ b. [The B-17] was hard to shoot down.

☐ c. The best defense the bombers had was to stick together.

3. The authors tell this story mainly by

☐ a. comparing different pilots' experiences.

☐ b. retelling people's personal experiences.

☐ c. using their imagination and creativity.

_____ Number of correct answers

Record your personal assessment of your work on the Critical Thinking Chart on page 104.

Summarizing and Paraphrasing

Follow the directions provided for the questions below.

1. Look for the important ideas and events in paragraphs 5 and 6. Summarize those paragraphs in one or two sentences.

_____

_____

_____

_____

2. Complete the following one-sentence summary of the article using the lettered phrases from the phrase bank below. Write the letters on the lines.

Phrase Bank

a. by telling about the award Lieutenant Michael received

b. a description of B-17 bombers

c. how Lieutenant Michael escaped the Germans

The article about Lieutenant Michael's amazing escape begins

with _____, goes on to explain _____, and ends _____.

3. Read the statement from the article below. Then read the paraphrase of that statement. Choose the reason that best tells why the paraphrase does not say the same thing as the statement.

Statement: The lumbering bomber was like a duck in a shooting gallery.

Paraphrase: The bomber would probably be shot down.

☐ a. Paraphrase says too much.

☐ b. Paraphrase doesn't say enough

☐ c. Paraphrase doesn't agree with the statement from the article.

_____ Number of correct answers

Record your personal assessment of your work on the Critical Thinking Chart on page 104.

Critical Thinking

Put an X in the box next to the correct answer for questions 1, 2, and 5. Follow the directions provided for questions 3 and 4.

1. Which of the following statements from the article is an opinion rather than a fact?

☐ a. The B-17 bomber had little ability to dodge enemy planes.

☐ b. He thought [parachuting] was their best chance of staying alive.

☐ c. He just pointed his plane northwest towards England and hoped the *Bertie Lee* made it there.

2. Based on what John Lieber said, you can conclude that he

☐ a. wasn't afraid when the *Bertie Lee* was hit.

☐ b. wanted to win a Medal of Honor.

☐ c. was loyal.

CRITICAL THINKING

3. Which paragraphs provide evidence from the article to support your answer to question 2? _____

4. Choose from the letters below to correctly complete the following statement. Write the letters on the lines.

   According to paragraph 16, _____ because _____.

   a.   the wheels didn't work without a hydraulic system

   b.   the bomb bay doors were stuck open

   c.   the plane had to land on its belly

5. What was the effect of Lieutenant Edward Michael's flying close to the ground?

   ☐ a.   Soldiers on the ground started firing at him.

   ☐ b.   Enemy fighters were waiting for him.

   ☐ c.   He made it to England.

   _____ Number of correct answers

   Record your personal assessment of your work on the Critical Thinking Chart on page 104.

Personal Response

I wonder why _____

_____

_____

_____

_____

Self-Assessment

What concepts or ideas from the article were difficult for you to understand?

_____

_____

_____

Which were easy to understand?

_____

_____

_____

Alone at Sea

Suppose you are lost at sea. You're floating on a raft in the middle of the ocean with no fresh water to drink. What should you do? Should you drink from the sea? If you do, will you go mad?

Will you die a terrible, agonizing death?

2   Over the years many sailors have been lost at sea. And most of them have refused to drink the salt water that was all around them. They believed they would die if they did. They thought drinking water from the ocean would drive them crazy with thirst and would hasten their deaths. Many knew of shipwrecked sailors who had, in desperation, consumed salt water. These men had been racked with terrible pains. They went out of their minds and finally died.

Dr. Alain Bombard crossed the Atlantic Ocean in this small raft to prove that people could survive indefinitely while drinking salt water.

3 Because of such tales, most stranded sailors avoided drinking even small amounts of salt water. They just waited in misery while their bodies slowly became dehydrated. A human being can live 30 days without food. But a person can live only 10 days without water.

4 Alain Bombard, a 27-year-old French doctor, wanted to save the lives of shipwrecked sailors. He felt it was a mistake for them not to drink seawater. In fact, he thought they should begin drinking it right away, before they became dehydrated. If they did that, he thought, their bodies could handle the extra salt. Then they could live much longer than 10 days.

5 To prove his point, Bombard decided to "shipwreck" himself. His plan was to drink a bit of seawater every day. Beyond that, he would get some water by squeezing the liquid out of fish he caught. Finally, he might pick up some rainwater here and there. Bombard was confident he could survive many days this way. But when he told people about his plan, they thought he was out of his mind.

6 On May 25, 1952, Bombard started his test. He cast himself adrift in the Mediterranean Sea in a rubber boat. A sailor named Jack Palmer went with him. The test was a flop. "The winds and currents drove us in circles for days," Bombard said. Worse still, the Mediterranean Sea didn't contain many fish. Bombard and Palmer had trouble catching enough to stay alive. Still, they survived more than two weeks. Drinking the salt water didn't make them crazy. But the voyage wasn't much fun.

7 Still, Bombard wasn't ready to give up. In fact, he wanted to try floating his raft across the entire Atlantic Ocean. Jack Palmer, on the other hand, had seen enough. He thought it would be suicide to head out across the ocean without fresh water.

8 So on October 19, 1952, Bombard set out across the Atlantic alone. He sailed in a 15-foot rubber boat. It had a wooden floor and a small mast. If Bombard made it all the way to the

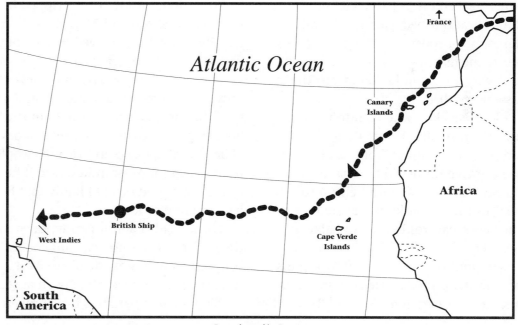

Bombard's Route

West Indies, he would have proved his theory. If he died, at least he felt his death would be for a noble cause.

9 Bombard did carry some food and water with him. He could use them to save his life. But if he did, his voyage would be a failure. To make sure no one could later claim he cheated, Bombard had officials lock the supplies with a special seal. If the seal was broken, everyone would know his theory had failed.

10 Other than these emergency supplies, Bombard took no food and no water. His food and drink would have to come from the sea. On this journey, he had no problem finding food. "There were plenty of fish," Bombard said. "Little flying fish struck against my sail and fell in the raft." He also fished with a makeshift harpoon. Of course, he had no stove. So he ate the fish raw. The pink flesh didn't look very good, but he found that the taste wasn't bad.

11 Bombard knew he couldn't live just on fish. If he did, he would get scurvy, a disease that comes from not getting the right vitamins. So Bombard dragged a piece of cloth behind the boat to catch plankton. Eating these tiny sea creatures helped to balance his diet.

12 For liquid, Bombard drank 1 $\frac{1}{2}$ pints of seawater each day. He also drank the juice he squeezed from fish. "For 23 days I had no rainwater, but fish juices served the purpose. I had no trouble with real thirst."

13 Bombard did, however, have trouble with loneliness. At times he was frightened by the "terror of the open sea." He longed for the sound of human voices. The only noises he heard during his journey were "the rushing of the wind, the watery hiss of the breaking waves, [and] the nervous flutter of the sail."

14 Early in his voyage, a storm almost destroyed his boat. Bombard had been sailing less than a week when the storm struck. Huge waves battered the boat. "One minute I perched atop [the waves] like a surfboard," he recalled, "the next, I was in a hollow so deep I could barely feel the wind." Strong winds ripped his sail. They also ruined his spare sail. Luckily, Bombard managed to sew the first sail back together again.

15 The next weeks passed quite uneventfully. Then, after about a month and a half, the wind suddenly died. Bombard's boat stopped moving. After several days of deadly calm, he began to fear he would never reach the West Indies. And if he died now, nobody would know that he had survived so long.

16 Then, at last, a British ship appeared on the horizon. The ship's captain couldn't believe Bombard was still alive. By this time the French doctor had been at sea for 53 days. Bombard was heartbroken to learn that he was still 600 miles from the West Indies. Still, he had proven his theory. According to the old belief, he should have died six weeks earlier.

17 Bombard could have ended his journey right then and there. But he wanted to continue on to the West Indies. So after a meager meal on board the ship, he climbed back into his boat. His spirits had been restored. Happily, the wind began to blow again.

18 On December 23, 1952, Dr. Alain Bombard reached the West Indies. He had been at sea for 65 days. He had sailed more than 2,750 miles and had lost 56 pounds. But he was alive. He had proven his theory! And, just in case someone doubted him, the seal on his emergency supplies was unbroken. 🐉

If you have been timed while reading this article, enter your reading time below. Then turn to the Words-per-Minute Table on page 101 and look up your reading speed (words per minute). Enter your reading speed on the graph on page 102.

Reading Time: Lesson 7

_____ : _____
Minutes   Seconds

A | Finding the Main Idea

One statement below expresses the main idea of the article. One statement is too general, or too broad. The other statement explains only part of the article; it is too narrow. Label the statements using the following key:

M—Main Idea   **B—Too Broad**   **N—Too Narrow**

_____ 1. By surviving a trip across the Atlantic Ocean eating and drinking only what he found in the sea, Dr. Alain Bombard proved that a person would not die from drinking salt water.

_____ 2. Dr. Alain Bombard believed that people could drink salt water and not die.

_____ 3. Dr. Alain Bombard's trip across the Atlantic Ocean lasted 65 days.

_____ Score 15 points for a correct M answer.

_____ Score 5 points for each correct B or N answer.

_____ **Total Score:** Finding the Main Idea

B | Recalling Facts

How well do you remember the facts in the article? Put an X in the box next to the answer that correctly completes each statement about the article.

1. Many people believed that drinking salt water would
☐ a. help a person to live 10 days.
☐ b. cause a person to go crazy and die.
☐ c. poison someone.

2. Dr. Alain Bombard believed that
☐ a. drinking seawater was good for the body.
☐ b. sailors should not drink seawater.
☐ c. if people began drinking seawater before they became dehydrated, their bodies could handle the extra salt.

3. When Bombard sailed across the Atlantic Ocean,
☐ a. he carried food and water in a sealed container only for emergency use.
☐ b. a sailor named Jack Palmer went with him.
☐ c. he carried no extra food or water.

4. To get vitamins while he was at sea, Bombard ate
☐ a. fish.
☐ b. fruit.
☐ c. plankton.

5. Bombard's biggest problem while he was at sea was
☐ a. loneliness.
☐ b. storms.
☐ c. thirst.

Score 5 points for each correct answer.

_____ **Total Score:** Recalling Facts

C Making Inferences

When you combine your own experience with information from a text to draw a conclusion that is not directly stated in that text, you are making an inference. Below are five statements that may or may not be inferences based on information in the article. Label the statements using the following key:

C—Correct Inference   **F—Faulty Inference**

_____ 1. People should drink salt water.

_____ 2. Drinking salt water in small quantities is safe.

_____ 3. Alain Bombard was an experienced sailor.

_____ 4. Bombard's raft did not have a motor.

_____ 5. Sailors crossing an ocean today usually drink salt water.

Score 5 points for each correct answer.

_____ **Total Score:** Making Inferences

D Using Words Precisely

Each numbered sentence below contains an underlined word or phrase from the article. Following the sentence are three definitions. One definition is closest to the meaning of the underlined word. One definition is opposite or nearly opposite. Label those two definitions using the following key; do not label the remaining definition.

C—Closest   **O—Opposite or Nearly Opposite**

1. They thought drinking water from the ocean would . . . <u>hasten</u> their deaths.

_____ a. speed up

_____ b. cause

_____ c. slow

2. They just waited in misery while their bodies slowly grew <u>dehydrated</u>.

_____ a. weak

_____ b. full of water

_____ c. dry

3. So he ate the fish <u>raw</u>.

_____ a. cooked

_____ b. uncooked

_____ c. whole

4. "I was in a <u>hollow</u> so deep I could barely feel the wind."

_____ a. hole

_____ b. whirlpool

_____ c. peak

5. So after a <u>meager</u> meal on board the ship, he climbed back into his boat.

_____ a. large

_____ b. small

_____ c. good

_____ Score 3 points for each correct C answer.

_____ Score 2 points for each correct O answer.

_____ **Total Score:** Using Words Precisely

Enter the four total scores in the spaces below, and add them together to find your Reading Comprehension Score. Then record your score on the graph on page 103.

Score	Question Type	Lesson 7
_____	Finding the Main Idea	
_____	Recalling Facts	
_____	Making Inferences	
_____	Using Words Precisely	
_____	**Reading Comprehension Score**	

Author's Approach

Put an X in the box next to the correct answer.

1. The main purpose of the first paragraph is to

☐ a. introduce the topic of the article.

☐ b. describe what happens when a person drinks salt water.

☐ c. inform the reader about salt water.

2. What is the authors' purpose in writing "Alone at Sea"?

☐ a. to express an opinion about Alain Bombard

☐ b. to describe Alain Bombard's journey

☐ c. to encourage the reader to drink salt water

3. From the statements below, choose the one that you believe the authors would agree with.

☐ a. Alain Bombard shouldn't have gone out to sea alone.

☐ b. Alain Bombard's discovery that people can survive after drinking salt water is very useful.

☐ c. Alain Bombard's experiment was interesting.

_____ Number of correct answers

Record your personal assessment of your work on the Critical Thinking Chart on page 104.

Summarizing and Paraphrasing

Put an X in the box next to the correct answer for questions 1 and 3. Follow the directions provided for question 2.

1. Below are summaries of the article. Choose the summary that says all the most important things about the article but in the fewest words.

☐ a. Dr. Alain Bombard believed that people could drink salt water and survive, and he proved it by crossing the Atlantic Ocean in a raft, eating and drinking only what he could find in the sea.

☐ b. Alain Bombard survived 65 days at sea drinking only salt water and eating fish and plankton.

☐ c. Although many people believed that they would die if they drank salt water, Dr. Alain Bombard believed that people could drink it and survive. To prove this, he "shipwrecked" himself twice, surviving only on what he could find in the sea. His second trip, which lasted 65 days, proved that people could survive by drinking salt water.

2. Reread paragraph 6 in the article. Below, write a summary of the paragraph in no more than 25 words.

_____

_____

_____

Reread your summary and decide whether it covers the important ideas in the paragraph. Next, decide how to shorten the summary to 15 words or less without leaving out any essential information. Write this summary below.

_____

_____

_____

3. Choose the best one-sentence paraphrase for the following sentence from the article: "At times he was frightened by the 'terror of the open sea.' "

☐ a. Sometimes he was afraid because he could see nothing but the sea all around him.

☐ b. Sometimes he was afraid of sharks, the terrors of the sea.

☐ c. Sometimes he was afraid of drowning in the sea.

_____ Number of correct answers

Record your personal assessment of your work on the Critical Thinking Chart on page 104.

Critical Thinking

Put an X in the box next to the correct answer for questions 1 and 5. Follow the directions provided for questions 2, 3, and 4.

1. Which of the following statements from the article is an opinion rather than a fact?

☐ a. [Bombard] felt it was a mistake for [sailors] not to drink seawater.

☐ b. To make sure no one could later claim he cheated, Bombard had officials lock the supplies with a special seal.

☐ c. Early in his voyage, a storm almost destroyed his boat.

2. Using the information in the article about Bombard's two "shipwrecks," list at least two ways in which they were similar and two ways in which they were different.

Similarities

_____

_____

_____

Differences

_____

_____

_____

3. Which paragraphs provide evidence from the article to support your answers to question 2? _____

4. Choose from the letters below to correctly complete the following statement. Write the letters on the lines.

   According to paragraph 15, _____ because _____.

   a.   Bombard's boat stopped moving

   b.   Bombard spotted a British ship

   c.   the wind suddenly died

5. What did you have to do to answer question 4?

   ☐   a.   find a description (how something looks)

   ☐   b.   find a cause (why something happened)

   ☐   c.   find a reason (why something is the way it is)

_____   Number of correct answers

Record your personal assessment of your work on the Critical Thinking Chart on page 104.

Personal Response

What new question do you have about this topic?

_____

_____

_____

Self-Assessment

I can't understand how _____

_____

_____

_____

Escape from Iran

Americans put up signs to thank Canadians for their help in getting six trapped Americans out of Iran.

It came as a total shock. No one is ever supposed to attack the embassy of another country. But that is what happened late in the morning of November 4, 1979. A mob of people filled the streets in Tehran, the capital city of Iran. They stormed the United States Embassy. They climbed over the walls and waved guns in the air. They shouted, "Death to America!"

2   In just a few minutes, the Iranians took control of the embassy. They captured 52 Americans there. These men and women would be held prisoners for the next 444 days. But six Americans escaped the mob. They

slipped out a back door. They ran into the street. They didn't know which way to turn. All they knew was that they were not safe. If anyone saw them, they would be taken hostage. They might even be killed.

3   Desperate, the six men and women went to the Canadian Embassy. They asked the Canadians to hide them. It was not a simple favor. If the Canadians agreed, they would be risking their own lives. The Iranians might find out. They might attack the Canadians.

4   Canada's Ambassador, Ken Taylor, knew that. He gathered his staff and told them about the dangers. Then he asked them what he should do. The Canadians didn't flinch. They wanted to help. Some even offered to hide Americans in their own homes. Taylor and his wife did this. They hid Joseph and Kathy Stafford.

5   Taylor's staff hoped to smuggle the six Americans out of Iran to safety. But how? The airports and train stations were closely watched. Any American trying to leave would be quickly arrested. So Taylor watched and waited. He sent some of his staff out of the country on unnecessary trips. He did this to find out how hard it would be to sneak someone out of Iran. He also wanted airport officials in Iran to get used to Canadians going in and out of the country.

6   Meanwhile, back in the United States, Antonio Mendez learned about the six men and women. Mendez worked for the CIA, America's spy agency. Mendez went to work on his own scheme for helping the six Americans. He talked to officials in Canada. He got them to issue six fake Canadian passports. The Americans would need these if they had any hope of slipping out of Iran.

7   Then Mendez dreamed up a bold plan. It was like something out of a movie. Mendez pretended to be an Irish filmmaker. He had to make Iranians believe he really was making a film. So he opened an office for his phony company. He hired people to work for it. Mendez decided his bogus film would be a science fiction thriller. He called it *Argo*. He created a script that called for some scenes to be shot in Tehran.

8   During this time, things remained tense for the six Americans and their Canadian hosts. All of them were afraid their secret would be discovered. On January 19, 1980, their fears came true. On that day Taylor's wife, Patricia, got a phone call.

9   "May I speak to Mr. or Mrs. Stafford?" the caller asked.

10   The question shook Patricia. No one knew that Joseph and Kathy Stafford were hiding in her house.

11   "I'm sorry," she said, trying to sound calm. "There is no one by that name living here."

12   But the caller repeated his question. He said he knew that the Staffords were there. At last, Patricia hung up.

13   The six Americans were now in great danger. They would have to get out of Iran, and they would have to move fast. The Canadians would have to clear out too. The Iranians might attack them for helping the Americans. Over the next few days, Taylor sent many of his staff members on trips out of Iran. None of them came back. Soon he had only four people left on his staff at the embassy.

14   At that point, Antonio Mendez showed up. He had gotten into Iran without any trouble. After all, his phony passport showed that he was Irish, not American. Mendez told

Iranian officials he had come to work on his film. But he told Taylor the truth. He had come to help get the six Americans out of the country.

15 Taylor got Mendez and the Americans together. Mendez gave them Canadian passports. He told them they were going to pose as members of his fake film company. Kathleen Stafford, for instance, would be the *Argo* set designer. Cora Lijek would be a screenwriter.

16 Mendez helped the Americans dress for their parts. He had Mark Lijek dye his beard black. He gave Kathleen Stafford a thick pair of glasses to wear. Bob Anders usually dressed in dark suits. But Mendez had him put on tight pants and a blue silk shirt that was open at the top. Mendez puffed up Anders's hair into a big wave. He put a flashy gold chain around his neck.

17 On January 28 the Americans went to the airport. Dressed as part of the *Argo* crew, they headed for a flight out of the country. As Mendez held his breath, they flashed their Canadian passports. The Iranians never gave them a second look. They all got on a plane for Germany and freedom. The same day, Taylor and his last three staff members quietly flew to Europe also.

18 It took the Iranians a while to figure out what had happened. When they did, they were furious. Their outrage was aimed at the Canadians. They branded Taylor and his staff outlaws. They even issued threats against Canada. A spokesman for Iran declared, "Sooner or later, somewhere in the world, Canada will pay for this crime."

19 To Americans, though, the Canadians were heroes. Taylor and his staff had risked their lives to help six frightened souls get out of Iran. Americans flooded the Canadian government with thank-you cards. They flew Canadian flags next to American ones. And all across the United States, people put up big signs that said, "Thank You, Canada."

20 It was years before the world found out that the CIA had also taken part in the scheme. Antonio Mendez had sworn an oath of secrecy. So no one knew what role he had played. No one stopped to shake his hand in the street. He got no signs or thank-you notes. And that was just fine with him. From his point of view, his daring actions had just been part of the job.

If you have been timed while reading this article, enter your reading time below. Then turn to the Words-per-Minute Table on page 101 and look up your reading speed (words per minute). Enter your reading speed on the graph on page 102.

Reading Time: Lesson 8

———— : ————
Minutes   *Seconds*

A Finding the Main Idea

One statement below expresses the main idea of the article. One statement is too general, or too broad. The other statement explains only part of the article; it is too narrow. Label the statements using the following key:

M—Main Idea   **B—Too Broad**   **N—Too Narrow**

_____ 1. To escape from Iran, a group of Americans pretended to be members of a fake film company.

_____ 2. When the United States Embassy in Tehran, Iran, was attacked in 1979, six Americans escaped.

_____ 3. When the United States Embassy in Tehran, Iran, was attacked, Canada's ambassador sheltered six Americans who had escaped and helped them get out of the country.

_____ Score 15 points for a correct M answer.

_____ Score 5 points for each correct B or N answer.

_____ **Total Score:** Finding the Main Idea

B Recalling Facts

How well do you remember the facts in the article? Put an X in the box next to the answer that correctly completes each statement about the article.

1. When the Iranians attacked the United States Embassy,
   ☐ a. they took 444 people prisoner.
   ☐ b. they killed 52 Americans.
   ☐ c. six Americans escaped.

2. Ken Taylor, the Canadian Ambassador, sent some of his staff out of the country on trips because
   ☐ a. he wanted to find out how hard it would be to sneak someone out of the country.
   ☐ b. he was afraid they would be arrested.
   ☐ c. the trips were necessary business trips.

3. When Antonio Mendez of the CIA learned about the six Americans, he
   ☐ a. issued them fake Canadian passports.
   ☐ b. came up with a plan to help them escape by posing as members of a fake film company.
   ☐ c. started filming a science fiction film called _Argo_.

4. Mendez had the Americans dress in costumes so that they
   ☐ a. wouldn't look like Americans.
   ☐ b. would look like people from Hollywood.
   ☐ c. wouldn't look like themselves.

5. No one knew that the CIA had helped with the escape because Mendez
   ☐ a. was not supposed to help.
   ☐ b. did not want to be considered a hero.
   ☐ c. had sworn an oath of secrecy.

Score 5 points for each correct answer.

_____ **Total Score:** Recalling Facts

C | Making Inferences

When you combine your own experience with information from a text to draw a conclusion that is not directly stated in that text, you are making an inference. Below are five statements that may or may not be inferences based on information in the article. Label the statements using the following key:

C—Correct Inference   **F—Faulty Inference**

_____ 1. In 1979 many Iranians did not like America.

_____ 2. The Canadian Embassy in Tehran is near the American Embassy.

_____ 3. All of the people taken hostage in the embassy attack were killed.

_____ 4. Antonio Mendez had helped people escape from hostile countries before.

_____ 5. Members of the CIA cannot talk about their work to people outside the organization.

Score 5 points for each correct answer.

_____ **Total Score:** Making Inferences

D | Using Words Precisely

Each numbered sentence below contains an underlined word or phrase from the article. Following the sentence are three definitions. One definition is closest to the meaning of the underlined word. One definition is opposite or nearly opposite. Label those two definitions using the following key; do not label the remaining definition.

C—Closest   **O—Opposite or Nearly Opposite**

1. If anyone saw them, they would be <u>taken hostage</u>.

_____ a. freed

_____ b. taken prisoner

_____ c. shot

2. So he opened an office for his <u>phony</u> company.

_____ a. real

_____ b. new

_____ c. fake

3. During this time, things remained <u>tense</u> for the six Americans and their Canadian hosts.

_____ a. exciting

_____ b. stressful

_____ c. relaxed

4. He put a <u>flashy</u> gold chain around his neck.

_____ a. ritzy

_____ b. shiny

_____ c. tasteful

5. Their <u>outrage</u> was aimed at the Canadians.

_____ a. emotion

_____ b. happiness

_____ c. anger

Enter the four total scores in the spaces below, and add them together to find your Reading Comprehension Score. Then record your score on the graph on page 103.

Score	Question Type	Lesson 8
_____	Finding the Main Idea	
_____	Recalling Facts	
_____	Making Inferences	
_____	Using Words Precisely	
_____	**Reading Comprehension Score**	

Author's Approach

Put an X in the box next to the correct answer.

1. The authors use the first sentence of the article to

☐ a. get the reader's attention.

☐ b. describe the embassy attack.

☐ c. entertain the reader.

2. What is the authors' purpose in writing "Escape from Iran"?

☐ a. to convey the Iranians' feelings towards America in 1979

☐ b. to describe how the Canadians helped six Americans escape from Iran

☐ c. to express an opinion about the Iranians' actions

3. From the statements below, choose the one that you believe the authors would agree with.

☐ a. Ken Taylor and Antonio Mendez's actions to help the six Americans were heroic.

☐ b. The Canadians should not have helped the Americans.

☐ c. The CIA should not have gotten involved in the situation.

_____ Number of correct answers

Record your personal assessment of your work on the Critical Thinking Chart on page 104.

CRITICAL THINKING

Summarizing and Paraphrasing

Follow the directions provided for the questions below.

1. Look for the important ideas and events in paragraphs 2 and 3. Summarize those paragraphs in one or two sentences.

_____

_____

_____

_____

2. Reread paragraph 13 in the article. Below, write a summary of the paragraph in no more than 25 words.

_____

_____

_____

_____

Reread your summary and decide whether it covers the important ideas in the paragraph. Next, decide how to shorten the summary to 15 words or less without leaving out any essential information. Write this summary below.

_____

_____

_____

3. Read the statement from the article below. Then read the paraphrase of that statement. Choose the reason that best tells why the paraphrase does not say the same thing as the statement.

Statement: It took the Iranians a while to figure out what had happened.

Paraphrase: At first, the Iranians didn't know what had happened.

☐ a. Paraphrase says too much.

☐ b. Paraphrase doesn't say enough.

☐ c. Paraphrase doesn't agree with the statement from the article.

_____ Number of correct answers

Record your personal assessment of your work on the Critical Thinking Chart on page 104.

Critical Thinking

Follow the directions provided for questions 1, 2, 3, and 5. Put an X in the box next to the correct answer for question 4.

1. For each statement below, write *O* if it expresses an opinion or *F* if it expresses a fact.

_____ a. No one is ever supposed to attack the embassy of another country.

_____ b. The Iranians might attack [the Canadians] for helping the Americans.

_____ c. Mendez told Iranian officials he had come to work on his film.

2. On the positive side, _____, but on the negative side
   _____.

   a. they didn't know where to go

   b. six Americans escaped when their embassy was attacked

   c. they went to the Canadian Embassy

3. Choose from the letters below to correctly complete the following statement. Write the letters on the lines.

   According to paragraph 6, _____ because _____.

   a. Mendez got the Americans fake Canadian passports

   b. he worked for the CIA

   c. they would need them to get out of Iran

4. What was the effect of the phone call to Patricia Taylor asking to speak to the Staffords?

   ☐ a. The Iranians had discovered that the Taylors were hiding the Staffords.

   ☐ b. The Canadians and Americans realized they had to leave Iran right away.

   ☐ c. The Iranians knew where the Staffords were hiding.

5. Which paragraphs provide evidence from the article to support

   your answer to question 4? _____

   _____ Number of correct answers

   Record your personal assessment of your work on the Critical Thinking Chart on page 104.

Personal Response

What was the most surprising or interesting to you about this article?

_____

_____

_____

_____

Self-Assessment

I can't really understand how _____

_____

_____

_____

_____

Fearless Reporter

One night in January 1995, Veronica Guerin heard a knock on the front door of her home in Dublin, Ireland. She opened the door. "The first thing my eyes were drawn to was a handgun," she said. Then she saw the man standing there, pointing the gun directly at her. "I looked up to his eyes to appeal to him—don't, don't shoot me." Then, expecting to die, she collapsed on the floor. The man pointed the gun at her head. But after a moment he lowered it and shot her in the thigh.

2   The bullet was meant to send a message. She had better stop writing

Veronica Guerin is pictured here with her son, Cathal, and her husband, Graham Turley.

about crime kingpins. Guerin was a reporter for the *Sunday Independent*, Ireland's most widely read newspaper. The day she was shot, one of her articles appeared. It was about a top criminal she called Monk. That wasn't his real name. Libel laws in Ireland are strict, so Guerin used nicknames. Still, it wasn't hard for people to figure out who Monk was.

3   The bullet in the thigh was not the first time some gangster tried to intimidate Guerin. In September 1994, she had written an article about the "General." This gangster had recently been shot dead in his car. Her story must have upset some members of his gang. About a month later, Guerin was playing with her young son at home. Suddenly, someone fired a bullet through her front window. Luckily, no one was hurt.

4   The bullet through the window had not stopped Guerin. And neither did the slug in her thigh. Veronica Guerin was not easily frightened. While still recovering from her leg wound, she left the hospital on crutches. Then she told her husband to drive her to see every big crime figure she knew. She

wanted to show them she couldn't be intimidated. "This is it," she explained to her husband. "I'm going to let [them] see they didn't get to me."

5   One threat, however, did almost get to her. Nine months after she was shot in the thigh she went to see John Gilligan, a mobster who had just gotten out of prison. She showed up at his lavish country estate without any notice. She asked Gilligan to explain how he could afford such a house. He had no job or any other legal source of wealth. Guerin's questions enraged Gilligan. He got so mad he ripped her shirt looking for a hidden microphone. He punched her in the face and chest. Then he screamed out a threat to kill her and her family.

6   Gilligan didn't stop there. The next day Guerin got a phone call from him. He whispered, "If you write one word about me, I will find your boy and kidnap him. I am going to shoot you, do you understand what I'm saying to you?" The direct threat to her 7-year-old son unnerved her. Still, she didn't quit investigating Gilligan.

7   In 1996 Guerin admitted that when she first started writing about drug

lords and other top criminals, she hadn't known how scary her job would turn out to be. If she had known, she said, "I would never have gotten into it. But having got into it, I cannot walk away from it. It's a job that must be done. And I'm a journalist."

8   Guerin believed her life was protected because she was a journalist. She didn't think any criminal would ever kill her. Yes, they might beat her and threaten her with death. But no journalist had ever been killed in Ireland. There seemed to be some unwritten rule against it. So when Liam Collins, one of Guerin's editors, cautioned her not to take wild risks, she just brushed him off. "Ah, come on," she said.

9   Meanwhile, Guerin won lots of praise from fellow journalists. "Veronica Guerin got close to criminals in a way that had never been done before," said Michael Foley of *The Irish Times*. That was why she got so many scoops—why so many of her stories made it to the front page.

10   After she was shot in the thigh, her newspaper put an expensive security system in her home. The police guarded her 24 hours a day. But that made it harder for Guerin to do her job. She couldn't get her informants to talk with the police around. Some of these people were small-time hoods. They didn't want to get near the police. But Guerin needed to talk to them in order to get information about the crime bosses. So she soon gave up her police escort. Later, she explained to her friends that no one could guarantee her safety. Even if she wore a bulletproof vest, she said, "I'd still have to take it off at night."

11   On June 26, 1996, Guerin had to go to court. She had recently gotten a ticket for speeding. She was worried that the judge might suspend her license. For Guerin, losing her license for three months or six months would have made her job difficult. Her car acted as a kind of mobile office. The judge, however, let Guerin off with a fine and a warning.

12   So Guerin was happy when she left the court. She headed back to the newspaper building. On the way, she stopped at a red light. As she waited she picked up her cell phone to call a friend. She didn't notice two men on a motorcycle pull up next to her. Suddenly, the man on the back of the bike jumped off. He pulled out a gun and fired five shots at her. The bullets smashed into her neck and chest. Veronica Guerin died instantly.

13   The murder shocked people around the world. John Bruton, the prime minister of Ireland, called the shooting "sinister in the extreme." The police launched a huge manhunt to find her killers. They put 60 detectives on the case. Guerin had made many enemies. So at first the police had a list of 150 suspects. It took them a while to find the right person.

14   In time, however, they arrested drug lord Paul Ward. In November 1998, he was tried and found guilty of murder. Ward was sentenced to life in prison.

If you have been timed while reading this article, enter your reading time below. Then turn to the Words-per-Minute Table on page 101 and look up your reading speed (words per minute). Enter your reading speed on the graph on page 102.

Reading Time: Lesson 9

——— : ———
Minutes   *Seconds*

A | Finding the Main Idea

One statement below expresses the main idea of the article. One statement is too general, or too broad. The other statement explains only part of the article; it is too narrow. Label the statements using the following key:

M—Main Idea   **B—Too Broad**   **N—Too Narrow**

_____ 1. Reporter Veronica Guerin was shot in the thigh because she wrote an article exposing a top criminal.

_____ 2. Veronica Guerin, a journalist who wrote stories exposing top criminals for Ireland's *Sunday Independent*, received many threats because of her work and was eventually murdered.

_____ 3. Veronica Guerin was a reporter for Ireland's *Sunday Independent* who wrote stories about top criminals.

_____ Score 15 points for a correct M answer.

_____ Score 5 points for each correct B or N answer.

_____ **Total Score:** Finding the Main Idea

B | Recalling Facts

How well do you remember the facts in the article? Put an X in the box next to the answer that correctly completes each statement about the article.

1. A man shot Veronica Guerin in the thigh because she
   ☐ a. had written an article about him.
   ☐ b. was a crime kingpin.
   ☐ c. had written an article about a criminal she called Monk.

2. A mobster named John Gilligan threatened Guerin because
   ☐ a. she had written an article about him.
   ☐ b. he had just gotten out of prison.
   ☐ c. she showed up at his house to ask him questions.

3. Guerin continued to write about criminals in spite of the threats because she
   ☐ a. thought it was a job that had to be done.
   ☐ b. wasn't afraid of the criminals.
   ☐ c. enjoyed talking to criminals.

4. Guerin did not want police protection because
   ☐ a. she did not think she would be killed.
   ☐ b. it made it harder for her to do her job.
   ☐ c. she wore a bulletproof vest.

5. Veronica Guerin was killed
   ☐ a. in a car accident.
   ☐ b. by John Gilligan.
   ☐ c. while she was in her car at a red light.

Score 5 points for each correct answer.

_____ **Total Score:** Recalling Facts

C **Making Inferences**

When you combine your own experience with information from a text to draw a conclusion that is not directly stated in that text, you are making an inference. Below are five statements that may or may not be inferences based on information in the article. Label the statements using the following key:

C—Correct Inference　　　**F—Faulty Inference**

_____ 1. The man who shot Guerin had been the subject of one of her articles.

_____ 2. Guerin enjoyed investigating criminals.

_____ 3. Guerin was friends with some of Ireland's top criminals.

_____ 4. Guerin was worried that her son would be harmed because of her career.

_____ 5. Guerin was not a good driver.

Score 5 points for each correct answer.

_____ **Total Score:** Making Inferences

 D **Using Words Precisely**

Each numbered sentence below contains an underlined word or phrase from the article. Following the sentence are three definitions. One definition is closest to the meaning of the underlined word. One definition is opposite or nearly opposite. Label those two definitions using the following key; do not label the remaining definition.

C—Closest　　　**O—Opposite or Nearly Opposite**

1. She had better stop writing about crime <u>kingpins</u>.

_____ a. victims

_____ b. followers

_____ c. bosses

2. The bullet in the thigh was not the first time some gangster tried to <u>intimidate</u> Guerin.

_____ a. scare

_____ b. hurt

_____ c. comfort

3. She showed up at his <u>lavish</u> country estate without any notice.

_____ a. quiet

_____ b. fancy

_____ c. run-down

4. Guerin's questions <u>enraged</u> Gilligan.

_____ a. angered

_____ b. pleased

_____ c. bothered

5. She was worried that the judge might <u>suspend</u> her license.

_____ a. continue

_____ b. lose

_____ c. take away

_____ Score 3 points for each correct C answer.

_____ Score 2 points for each correct O answer.

_____ **Total Score:** Using Words Precisely

Enter the four total scores in the spaces below, and add them together to find your Reading Comprehension Score. Then record your score on the graph on page 103.

Score	Question Type	Lesson 9
_____	Finding the Main Idea	
_____	Recalling Facts	
_____	Making Inferences	
_____	Using Words Precisely	
_____	**Reading Comprehension Score**	

Author's Approach

Put an X in the box next to the correct answer.

1. The main purpose of the first paragraph is to

☐ a. entertain the reader.

☐ b. introduce Veronica Guerin.

☐ c. get the reader's attention.

2. What is the authors' purpose in writing "Fearless Reporter"?

☐ a. to inform the reader about Veronica Guerin

☐ b. to inform the reader about organized crime in Ireland

☐ c. to describe Veronica Guerin's death

3. The authors tell this story mainly by

☐ a. writing about different crime kingpins.

☐ b. retelling Veronica Guerin's experiences.

☐ c. using their imagination and creativity.

_____ Number of correct answers

Record your personal assessment of your work on the Critical Thinking Chart on page 104.

Summarizing and Paraphrasing

Follow the directions provided for questions 1 and 3. Put an X in the box next to the correct answer for question 2.

1. Look for the important ideas and events in paragraphs 5 and 6. Summarize those paragraphs in one or two sentences.

_____

_____

_____

_____

2. Below are summaries of the article. Choose the summary that says all the most important things about the article but in the fewest words.

☐ a. Veronica Guerin was a newspaper reporter in Ireland who wrote about crime kingpins and was eventually murdered by one of them.

☐ b. Veronica Guerin received several death threats because of her work reporting on top criminals.

☐ c. Veronica Guerin, an Irish reporter who wrote stories exposing top criminals, received several death threats because of her work and was eventually murdered by one of the crime kingpins.

3. Read the statement from the article below. Then read the paraphrase of that statement. Choose the reason that best tells why the paraphrase does not say the same thing as the statement.

Statement: "The direct threat to her 7-year-old son unnerved her."

Paraphrase: Guerin worried about her son.

☐ a. Paraphrase says too much.

☐ b. Paraphrase doesn't say enough.

☐ c. Paraphrase doesn't agree with the statement from the article.

> _____ Number of correct answers
>
> Record your personal assessment of your work on the Critical Thinking Chart on page 104.

Critical Thinking

Follow the directions provided for questions 1, 3, 4, and 5. Put an X in the box next to the correct answer for question 2.

1. For each statement below, write *O* if it expresses an opinion or *F* if it expresses a fact.

_____ a. The bullet in the thigh was not the first time some gangster tried to intimidate Guerin.

_____ b. [Guerin] didn't think any criminal would ever kill her.

_____ c. For Guerin, losing her license for three months or six months would have made her job difficult.

2. From the information in the article, you can conclude that

☐ a. since Guerin's murder, no one reports on crime kingpins in Ireland.

☐ b. since Guerin's murder, more reporters have been murdered for reporting on crime kingpins.

☐ c. Paul Ward was the subject of one of Guerin's articles.

3. Which paragraphs provide evidence from the article to support your answer to question 2? _____

4. Use the information in the article to list at least two ways in which the threats to Veronica Guerin's life by "Monk" and John Gilligan were similar and two ways in which they were different.

Similarities

_____

_____

_____

Differences

_____

_____

_____

5. Choose from the letters below to correctly complete the following statement. Write the letters on the lines.

According to paragraph 4, _____ because _____.

a. she wanted them to know she wasn't afraid

b. Guerin went to visit top crime figures while she was on crutches

c. Guerin left the hospital on crutches

_____ Number of correct answers

Record your personal assessment of your work on the Critical Thinking Chart on page 104.

Personal Response

How do you think Veronica Guerin felt when John Gilligan threatened her son?

_____

_____

_____

_____

Self-Assessment

From reading this article, I have learned _____

_____

_____

Nurses on the Front Line

During World War II, nurses were on the front lines just like the soldiers. Here, Red Cross nurses march in formation.

They got sick just like the men. They were bombed and shot at just like the men. And they were taken prisoners of war just like the men. During World War II, American army nurses were right up on the front lines. About the only difference between a male soldier and a female nurse was that the nurse did not carry a gun.

2. Nurses in the Philippines had a particularly tough time. By late 1941, 88 U.S. Army nurses were stationed there. On December 8 of that year, Japan attacked the islands. It was not a fair match. The Japanese had more men, planes, and ships. Yet the Americans fought bravely to hold out as long as they could.

3. During the intense fighting, the nurses worked hard to do their jobs.

4. Every day more and more men were brought to the two emergency hospitals. These "hospitals" were nothing more than tents. Even so, there was not room in them for all the wounded men. Some had to be treated out in the open.

5. Living conditions in the Philippines were awful. The water was filthy. Almost everyone got sick. The Americans endured everything from hookworm to dengue fever. The nurses had begun their work dressed in starched white uniforms. Before long, they switched to baggy overalls. Food was scarce. So rations were cut in half. Then they were cut to three-eighths. People started eating whatever they could find. They ate roots, leaves, monkeys, and pigs.

6. On March 29, 1942, enemy planes bombed one of the hospitals. A nurse recalled what it was like. "The sergeant pulled me under the desk," she said. "The desk was blown into the air, and he and I with it. . . . Then I fell back to the floor, and the desk landed on top of me."

7. The sergeant pushed the desk off the nurse. She struggled to her feet and looked around. She was appalled by what she saw. Two nurses had been wounded. More than 100 patients had been hurt or killed. Some had been blown out of their beds. Severed arms and legs lay all over. Some of these limbs were hanging from nearby tree branches.

8. This attack was followed by others. The nurses knew they could do nothing about it. All they could do was care for the wounded and hope for the best.

9. In early April the Americans suffered a major loss. Thousands were taken prisoner by the Japanese. A few nurses were captured. The rest joined troops who were fleeing to the island of Corregidor. Hattie Brantley was one of the nurses who fled. She did not want to leave her patients. She did so only when she heard the shouts of Japanese soldiers coming up over the hill toward her. She and other nurses escaped in buses as bombs burst all around them.

10. By April 8 the only part of the Philippines that Americans still held was Corregidor. This island had several tunnels. About 13,000 men and women

hid in them. The tunnels were safer than tents. But that was little comfort. The tunnels were hot, dark, and noisy. The nurses had to work by flashlight. "We were like a bunch of rats in a hole," said nurse Minnie Stubbs. Each day shells blasted the land overhead. "The shelling shook the whole mountain," said Stubbs.

11   At last, on May 6, the remaining Americans surrendered. Japan now had full control of the Philippines. Sixty-seven nurses became prisoners of war, or POWs. They were sent to a prison camp called Santo Tomas. There they stayed for three grueling years.

12   Life as a POW was brutal. The Japanese had strict rules for the prisoners. Anyone who broke them was punished. Many prisoners were beaten for lying or for trying to escape.

13   The nurses were sick and hungry when they got to the prison camp. Once there, things got worse. Each day they struggled to get enough to eat. Each person was given a cup of rice twice a day. To eat it, they first had to pick the bugs out. Beyond that, the prisoners got nothing. Luckily, they managed to grow some food for themselves. Often they were so eager for something green that they ate the leaves of the potatoes as soon as they appeared.

14   The nurses did what they could for the sick and wounded men who were kept in the prison camp with them. But the nurses had few clean bandages and few medicines. They gave patients aspirin and vitamin pills. But mostly they offered TLC—tender loving care. They washed faces, held hands, and talked.

15   The POWs received no news from the outside world. So they had no way of knowing which side was winning the war. Still, they kept their hopes up. Often they climbed trees to look out over the sea. They hoped to see a fleet of American ships. "It was a matter of faith," said Hattie Brantley. "We really believed that if we could get through today, help would be there tomorrow."

16   As time passed, conditions at the camp grew steadily worse. By late 1944 the food ran out. There was no longer even rice for them to eat. The POWs scrounged whatever they could. They ate "dogs, frogs, and even rats."

17   More and more of the prisoners died of starvation. But help was on the way. On February 3, 1945, American troops liberated the POWs at Santo Tomas. One of the nurses had saved a bottle of Coke all this time. To lift morale, she sometimes would take it out of hiding and show it. On this day, she celebrated by finally opening it up. She and all the other ex-POWs stood together and sang "God Bless America."

18   Amazingly, all of the nurses had survived their years in the prison camp. Their courage and kindness helped other prisoners survive as well. For their heroism in the line of duty, each nurse was promoted. And each received the Bronze Star, one of the highest honors given out by the U.S. Army.

If you have been timed while reading this article, enter your reading time below. Then turn to the Words-per-Minute Table on page 101 and look up your reading speed (words per minute). Enter your reading speed on the graph on page 102.

Reading Time: Lesson 10

_____ : _____
Minutes   *Seconds*

A Finding the Main Idea

One statement below expresses the main idea of the article. One statement is too general, or too broad. The other statement explains only part of the article; it is too narrow. Label the statements using the following key:

M—Main Idea   **B—Too Broad**   **N—Too Narrow**

_____ 1. Nurses serving in World War II were bombed, shot at, and taken prisoner just like the soldiers.

_____ 2. Nurses serving in World War II suffered a lot of hardships.

_____ 3. Some nurses serving in the Philippines during World War II were captured and sent to Japanese prison camps for three years.

_____ Score 15 points for a correct M answer.

_____ Score 5 points for each correct B or N answer.

_____ **Total Score:** Finding the Main Idea

B Recalling Facts

How well do you remember the facts in the article? Put an X in the box next to the answer that correctly completes each statement about the article.

1. Unlike soldiers, nurses serving in World War II
   ☐ a. were not on the front lines.
   ☐ b. did not carry guns.
   ☐ c. were not taken prisoner.

2. While they were serving in the Philippines, army nurses
   ☐ a. did not have enough to eat.
   ☐ b. wore starched white uniforms.
   ☐ c. enjoyed eating monkeys.

3. When the American army retreated to the island of Corregidor, the soldiers and nurses
   ☐ a. worked in tents.
   ☐ b. hid in the mountains.
   ☐ c. hid in underground tunnels.

4. The prisoners at Santo Tomas were
   ☐ a. given dogs to eat.
   ☐ b. only given rice to eat.
   ☐ c. given medical supplies.

5. The nurses who were sent to Santo Tomas
   ☐ a. were each awarded the Bronze Star, one of the army's highest awards.
   ☐ b. left the army after being rescued.
   ☐ c. did not survive.

Score 5 points for each correct answer.

_____ **Total Score:** Recalling Facts

Making Inferences

When you combine your own experience with information from a text to draw a conclusion that is not directly stated in that text, you are making an inference. Below are five statements that may or may not be inferences based on information in the article. Label the statements using the following key:

C—Correct Inference   F—Faulty Inference

_____ 1. Nurses did not fight during World War II.

_____ 2. The American Army had built the tunnels on Corregidor to protect their forces.

_____ 3. All of the army nurses during World War II were women.

_____ 4. The Japanese killed many of their prisoners.

_____ 5. The Bronze Star is given to prisoners of war who survive.

Score 5 points for each correct answer.

_____ **Total Score:** Making Inferences

D **Using Words Precisely**

Each numbered sentence below contains an underlined word or phrase from the article. Following the sentence are three definitions. One definition is closest to the meaning of the underlined word. One definition is opposite or nearly opposite. Label those two definitions using the following key; do not label the remaining definition.

C—Closest   O—Opposite or Nearly Opposite

1. The Americans <u>endured</u> everything from hookworm to dengue fever.

_____ a. enjoyed

_____ b. suffered

_____ c. saw

2. Food was <u>scarce</u>.

_____ a. bad

_____ b. plentiful

_____ c. not enough

3. The rest joined troops who were <u>fleeing</u> to the island of Corregidor.

_____ a. sailing

_____ b. running away

_____ c. coming

4. There they stayed for three <u>grueling</u> years.

_____ a. comfortable

_____ b. long

_____ c. very difficult

5. On February 3, 1945, American troops <u>liberated</u> the POWs at Santo Tomas.

_____ a. found

_____ b. captured

_____ c. freed

_____ Score 3 points for each correct C answer.

_____ Score 2 points for each correct O answer.

_____ **Total Score:** Using Words Precisely

Enter the four total scores in the spaces below, and add them together to find your Reading Comprehension Score. Then record your score on the graph on page 103.

Score	Question Type	Lesson 10
_____	Finding the Main Idea	
_____	Recalling Facts	
_____	Making Inferences	
_____	Using Words Precisely	
_____	**Reading Comprehension Score**	

Author's Approach

Put an X in the box next to the correct answer.

1. The main purpose of the first paragraph is to

☐ a. introduce the topic of the article.

☐ b. describe the nurses who served in World War II.

☐ c. compare nurses and soldiers.

2. What is the authors' purpose in writing "Nurses on the Front Line"?

☐ a. to describe the conditions in the Philippines during World War II

☐ b. to emphasize the similarities between nurses and soldiers during World War II

☐ c. to inform the reader about the role of nurses during World War II

3. What do the authors mean by the statement, "[The nurses'] courage and kindness helped other prisoners survive as well."

☐ a. The nurses helped other prisoners to escape the prison camp.

☐ b. The nurses were kind to everyone in the prison camp.

☐ c. The nurses' work and example gave other prisoners hope and reason to continue living.

_____ Number of correct answers

Record your personal assessment of your work on the Critical Thinking Chart on page 104.

Summarizing and Paraphrasing

Follow the directions provided for questions 1 and 2. Put an X in the box next to the correct answer for question 3.

1. Reread paragraph 4 in the article. Below, write a summary of the paragraph in no more than 25 words.

_____

_____

_____

Reread your summary and decide whether it covers the important ideas in the paragraph. Next, decide how to shorten the summary to 15 words or less without leaving out any essential information. Write this summary below.

_____

_____

_____

2. Complete the following one-sentence summary of the article using the lettered phrases from the phrase bank below. Write the letters on the lines.

Phrase Bank
a. a description of their work
b. what happened after their rescue
c. how they were captured and conditions in the prison camp

The article about nurses serving in World War II begins with

_____, goes on to explain _____, and ends by telling

_____.

3. Choose the sentence that correctly restates the following sentence from the article: "During the intense fighting, the nurses worked hard to do their job."

☐ a. The nurses worked hard while the men were fighting.

☐ b. The nurses had to work harder when there was more fighting.

☐ c. During difficult battles it was harder for nurses to do their jobs.

_____ Number of correct answers

Record your personal assessment of your work on the Critical Thinking Chart on page 104.

Critical Thinking

Put an X in the box next to the correct answer for questions 1, 2, and 5. Follow the directions provided for questions 3 and 4.

1. Which of the following statements from the article is an opinion rather than a fact?

☐ a. More and more of the prisoners died of starvation.

☐ b. The Japanese had strict rules for the prisoners.

☐ c. "We really believed that if we could get through today, help would be there tomorrow."

2. From the information in the article, you can conclude that

☐ a. no nurses died during World War II.

☐ b. the army could only get a limited amount of food to the Philippines.

☐ c. nurses were not usually taken prisoner during World War II.

3. Choose from the letters below to correctly complete the following statement. Write the letters on the lines.

   According to the article, the surrender of the Americans at Corregidor caused _____ to _____, and the effect was that _____.

   a. be captured by the Japanese

   b. they were sent to the Santo Tomas prison camp

   c. 67 nurses

4. In which paragraph did you find the information to answer question 3? _____

5. Into which of the following theme categories would this story best fit?

   ☐ a. bravery in battle

   ☐ b. the horrors of war

   ☐ c. the history of the Philippines

   _____ Number of correct answers

   Record your personal assessment of your work on the Critical Thinking Chart on page 104.

Personal Response

I can't believe _____

_____

_____

_____

_____

Self-Assessment

From reading this article, I have learned _____

_____

_____

_____

_____

Compare and Contrast

Think about the articles you have read in Unit Two. Pick the three articles you thought showed the most useful jobs. Write the titles of the articles in the first column of the chart below. Use information you have learned from the articles to fill in the empty boxes in the chart.

Title	What is the job of the central person in this article?	Why is this job useful? What useful things did the people mentioned in the article do?	What would be the most difficult part of doing this job?

Which of the jobs above do you think you would be best at? _____ Why? _____

_____

_____

Words-per-Minute Table

Unit Two

Directions: If you were timed while reading an article, refer to the Reading Time you recorded in the box at the end of the article. Use this Words-per-Minute Table to determine your reading speed for that article. Then plot your reading speed on the graph on page 102.

Lesson No. of Words	6 1,108	7 1,098	8 1,098	9 1,033	10 1,010	Seconds
1:30	739	732	732	689	673	90
1:40	665	659	659	620	606	100
1:50	604	599	599	563	551	110
2:00	554	549	549	517	505	120
2:10	511	507	507	477	466	130
2:20	475	471	471	443	433	140
2:30	443	439	439	413	404	150
2:40	416	412	412	387	379	160
2:50	391	388	388	365	356	170
3:00	369	366	366	344	337	180
3:10	350	347	347	326	319	190
3:20	332	329	329	310	303	200
3:30	317	314	314	295	289	210
3:40	302	299	299	282	275	220
3:50	289	286	286	269	263	230
4:00	277	275	275	258	253	240
4:10	266	264	264	248	242	250
4:20	256	253	253	238	233	260
4:30	246	244	244	230	224	270
4:40	237	235	235	221	216	280
4:50	229	227	227	214	209	290
5:00	222	220	220	207	202	300
5:10	214	213	213	200	195	310
5:20	208	206	206	194	189	320
5:30	201	200	200	689	184	330
5:40	196	194	194	182	178	340
5:50	190	188	188	177	173	350
6:00	185	183	183	172	168	360
6:10	180	178	178	168	164	370
6:20	175	173	173	620	159	380
6:30	170	169	169	159	155	390
6:40	166	165	165	155	152	400
6:50	162	161	161	151	148	410
7:00	158	157	157	148	144	420
7:10	155	153	153	144	141	430
7:20	151	150	150	141	138	440
7:30	148	146	146	138	135	450
7:40	145	143	143	135	132	460
7:50	141	140	140	132	129	470
8:00	139	137	137	129	126	480

Minutes and Seconds

Plotting Your Progress: Reading Speed

Unit Two

Directions: If you were timed while reading an article, write your words-per-minute rate for that article in the box under the number of the lesson. Then plot your reading speed on the graph by putting a small X on the line directly above the number of the lesson, across from the number of words per minute you read. As you mark your speed for each lesson, graph your progress by drawing a line to connect the X's.

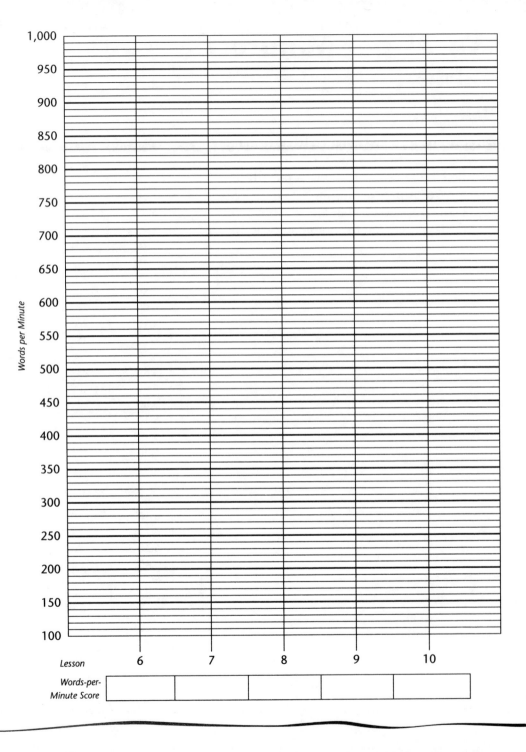

Lesson	6	7	8	9	10
Words-per-Minute Score					

Plotting Your Progress: Reading Comprehension

Unit Two

Directions: Write your Reading Comprehension Score for each lesson in the box under the number of the lesson. Then plot your score on the graph by putting a small X on the line directly above the number of the lesson and across from the score you earned. As you mark your score for each lesson, graph your progress by drawing a line to connect the X's.

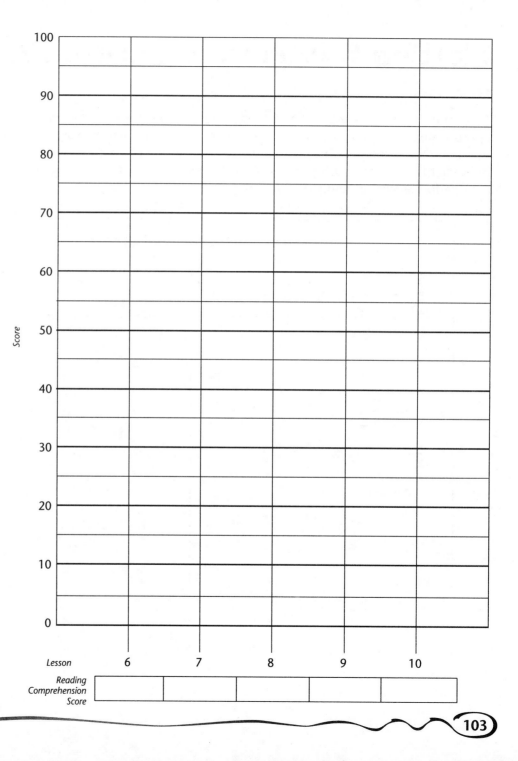

Plotting Your Progress: Critical Thinking

Unit Two

Directions: Work with your teacher to evaluate your responses to the Critical Thinking questions for each lesson. Then fill in the appropriate spaces in the chart below. For each lesson and each type of Critical Thinking question, do the following: Mark a minus sign (–) in the box to indicate areas in which you feel you could improve. Mark a plus sign (+) to indicate areas in which you feel you did well. Mark a minus-slash-plus sign (–/+) to indicate areas in which you had mixed success. Then write any comments you have about your performance, including ideas for improvement.

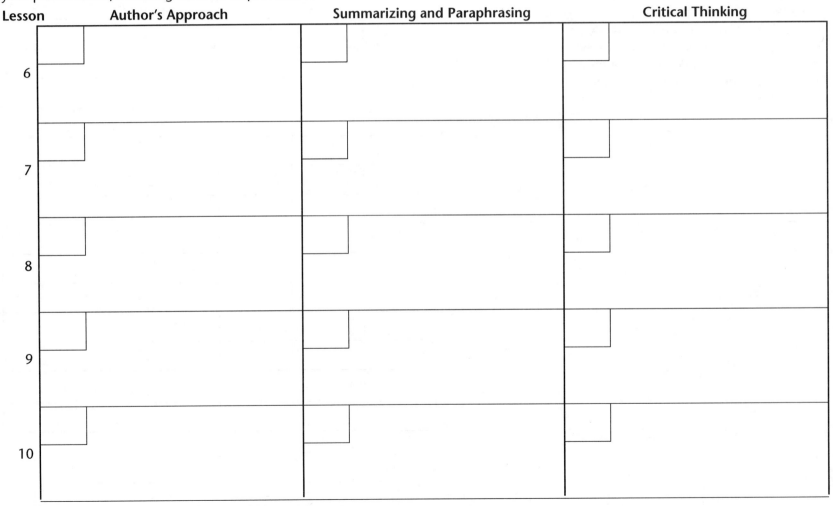

Lesson	Author's Approach	Summarizing and Paraphrasing	Critical Thinking
6			
7			
8			
9			
10			

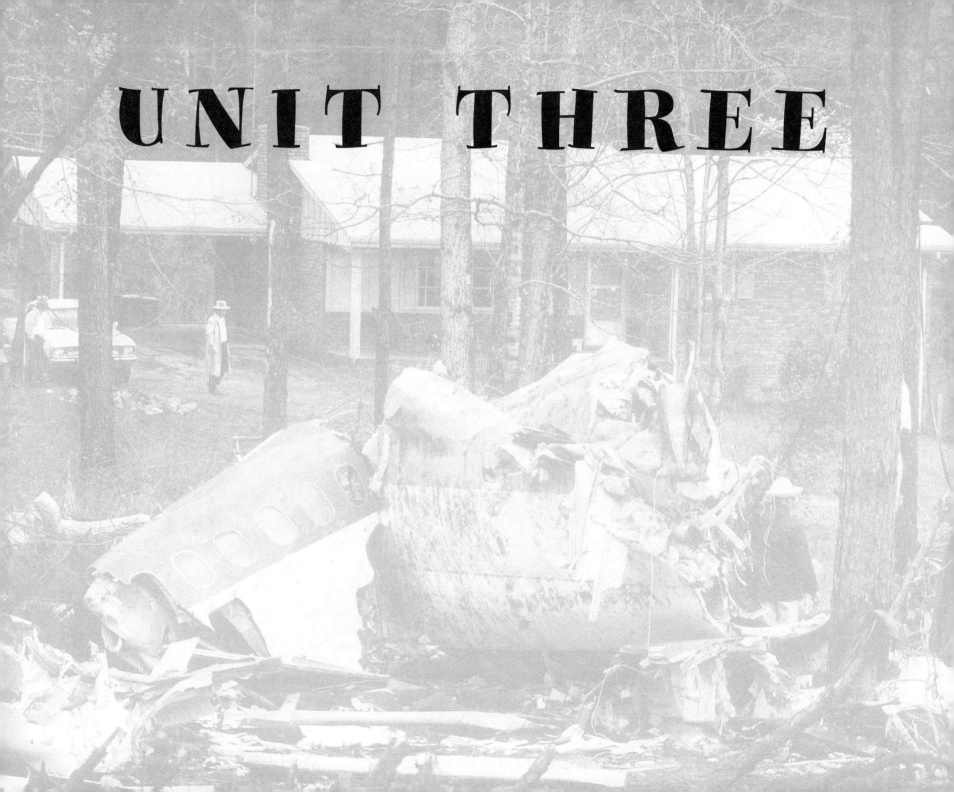

UNIT THREE

Life and Death: The Crash of Flight 242

"Bend down and grab your ankles," ordered Sandy Purl. The 81 passengers, who were buckled into their seats, did as they were told.

2   Purl was a flight attendant aboard Southern Airways Flight 242. She wanted the passengers to be prepared. Purl knew the DC-9 twin engine jet was in trouble. The windshield in the cockpit had been cracked by hail. And moments earlier she had smelled smoke.

3   As Purl gave instructions to the passengers, she walked back to her seat. Then she clamped on her seat belt. She braced herself for a crash landing.

Southern Airways flight 242 crashed in the yard of a home near New Hope, Georgia.

4   It was April 4, 1977. Purl was one of a four-person crew. The others were Captain William McKenzie, his copilot Lyman Keele, and flight attendant Cathy Lemoine. For the past two days, these four men and women had worked as a team on a series of short flights. They had just two hops left. First they were to fly from Huntsville, Alabama, to Atlanta, Georgia. Then they would continue on to New Orleans, Louisiana. The distance from Huntsville to Atlanta was only 150 miles. It was on this short flight, however, that things went wrong.

5   The DC-9 had climbed to 17,000 feet. A storm of rain and heavy hail began to batter the plane. High winds made the jet bounce wildly. Purl heard three loud bangs in the left engine. The cabin lights flickered and went out. A few moments later, the lights came back on again. Purl picked up her microphone. She knew she needed to calm the passengers. "Keep your seat belts securely fastened," she said reassuringly. "There's nothing to be alarmed about. Relax. We should be out of the storm shortly."

6   But suddenly Purl smelled smoke. That's when she realized the plane was in serious trouble. Unbuckling her seat belt, she walked to the passengers who were sitting next to the exit windows. She talked softly to them. She had to be sure they knew what to do if the plane made a crash landing.

7   Purl didn't know it, but the loud noises she'd heard meant that the left engine had died. Soon the right engine stopped working as well. This was the first time such a thing had happened to a DC-9. In 112 million hours of flying time, no DC-9 engine had ever failed in a rainstorm. But in this case, huge amounts of rain and hail had been sucked into the engines. Both of them malfunctioned at almost the same instant.

8   While Sandy Purl tried to keep the passengers calm, Captain McKenzie struggled to land the plane safely. He knew he'd never make it to the airport in Atlanta. He couldn't even make it to Dobbins Air Force base just 15 miles away. In fact, McKenzie knew he couldn't make it to any airport. He had to land the plane right away. But where?

9   His best chance seemed to be Route 92 near New Hope, Georgia. He aimed the plane for this two-lane highway. As

the plane descended, its wings clipped trees, road signs, and telephone poles. The jet smashed into three cars. It took the roof off a local grocery store. Then, as it veered into the woods, it erupted in a ball of flames. It finally stopped moving 200 yards from the road.

10   Ruby Shipp, who lived across the highway, heard the crash. At first she thought it was thunder. "I thought, Lord, it's the tornado they were talking about on the television," she said. "I looked out and it was a solid black cloud of smoke. But I saw it was not a tornado. It was a plane on fire."

11   The crash killed nine people on the ground. It also killed many people on board. But not everyone on the plane died. Purl survived the crash in relatively good shape. When the plane stopped, however, she saw nothing but a wall of flames ahead of her. She tried to get out the back exit. But the door wouldn't open.

12   Purl feared she was trapped. She knew poison fumes from the fire would kill her in less than a minute. So she shielded her face with her arm and scrambled for the front exit. Fortunately, it was open and she was able to hop out onto the ground.

13   As she moved away from the wreckage, she looked back. The part of the plane where she had been sitting suddenly exploded. Pieces of metal

went flying through the air. She could smell burning jet fuel as well as burning flesh.

14   As the shock of the crash began to wear off, Purl's mind turned to the passengers. She realized some of them might still be alive. She saw one badly burned man lying on the ground. She pulled him away from the flames. After getting him to the safety of the road, Purl rushed back to the burning wreckage. She saw another passenger with his suit on fire. Purl knocked him to the ground, rolling him over and over until she had snuffed out the flames.

15   By this time, rescue workers were beginning to arrive. One of them tried to lead Purl away from the crash site. But she protested and raced back to the plane to look for more survivors. The only thought she had was what she had learned in her safety training: "You are responsible for your passengers."

16   As Purl picked through the sheets of hot metal, she enlisted several other surviving passengers to help her. She got bystanders to cover the people who were burned. And she told others how to care for those in shock.

17   During this time, Purl never noticed how badly her own feet were cut. In fact, she was functioning in a daze. Her mind could not absorb the horror. At one point she asked an ambulance

nurse, "Am I alive?" The nurse said yes. But Purl only half believed her. This nurse wanted Purl to go to the hospital with the other survivors, but Purl refused. She wanted to find the rest of the crew.

18   Then Purl spotted the remains of the cockpit. Walking over to it, she saw the bodies of Captain McKenzie and copilot Keele. At that point, there was little left for her to do.

19   In all, the crash of Southern Airways Flight 242 killed 63 people. But there was some good news for Purl. Flight attendant Cathy Lemoine survived. She, too, helped to save some of the passengers. Thanks in part to these women's courage and sense of duty, 20 passengers survived the crash.

If you have been timed while reading this article, enter your reading time below. Then turn to the Words-per-Minute Table on page 147 and look up your reading speed (words per minute). Enter your reading speed on the graph on page 148.

Reading Time: Lesson 11

————— : —————
Minutes   Seconds

A Finding the Main Idea

One statement below expresses the main idea of the article. One statement is too general, or too broad. The other statement explains only part of the article; it is too narrow. Label the statements using the following key:

M—Main Idea   **B—Too Broad**   **N—Too Narrow**

_____ 1. Southern Airways Flight 242 crashed when both of its engines stopped working while flying through a rainstorm.

_____ 2. When Captain William McKenzie realized he had to land his plane right away, he decided to land it on Route 92, a two-lane highway in Georgia.

_____ 3. When the plane she was in crashed and burned after both of its engines failed, flight attendant Sandy Purl remained focused on helping passengers.

_____ Score 15 points for a correct M answer.

_____ Score 5 points for each correct B or N answer.

_____ **Total Score:** Finding the Main Idea

B Recalling Facts

How well do you remember the facts in the article? Put an X in the box next to the answer that correctly completes each statement about the article.

1. Flight attendant Sandy Purl knew the airplane was in trouble when
   ☐ a. the lights went out in the cockpit.
   ☐ b. she smelled smoke.
   ☐ c. high winds made the jet bounce wildly.

2. The three loud bangs Purl heard meant that
   ☐ a. both engines had stopped working.
   ☐ b. water had gotten into the left engine.
   ☐ c. the left engine had died.

3. Captain McKenzie decided to land the plane on Route 92 because
   ☐ a. he had to land the plane right away and wasn't close enough to an airport.
   ☐ b. it was wider than most runways.
   ☐ c. it served as a runway for Dobbins Air Force base.

4. As the plane was landing on Route 92, it
   ☐ a. flew through a tornado.
   ☐ b. clipped trees, road signs, and telephone poles.
   ☐ c. smashed into nine cars.

5. After escaping the wreckage, Sandy Purl
   ☐ a. was taken to the hospital.
   ☐ b. immediately went to look for the other crew members.
   ☐ c. searched for and helped several passengers.

Score 5 points for each correct answer.

_____ **Total Score:** Recalling Facts

C | Making Inferences

When you combine your own experience with information from a text to draw a conclusion that is not directly stated in that text, you are making an inference. Below are five statements that may or may not be inferences based on information in the article. Label the statements using the following key:

C—Correct Inference　　　　　　**F—Faulty Inference**

_____　1. DC-9s are not reliable airplanes.

_____　2. Pilots are taught to land on a road if they cannot make it to an airport.

_____　3. Flight attendants are trained on what to do in emergency situations.

_____　4. Purl had been in a plane that had crash-landed before.

_____　5. The pilot and copilot died in the crash.

> Score 5 points for each correct answer.
>
> _____ **Total Score:** Making Inferences

D | Using Words Precisely

Each numbered sentence below contains an underlined word or phrase from the article. Following the sentence are three definitions. One definition is closest to the meaning of the underlined word. One definition is opposite or nearly opposite. Label those two definitions using the following key; do not label the remaining definition.

C—Closest　　　　**O—Opposite or Nearly Opposite**

1. The cabin lights <u>flickered</u> and went out.

_____　a. blinked

_____　b. stayed on

_____　c. dimmed

2. "There's nothing to be <u>alarmed</u> about."

_____　a. worried

_____　b. angry

_____　c. calm

3. Both of them <u>malfunctioned</u> at almost the same instant.

_____　a. flooded

_____　b. broke down

_____　c. kept working

4. As the plane <u>descended</u>, its wings clipped trees, road signs, and telephone poles.

_____　a. climbed

_____　b. flew

_____　c. came down

5. Then, as it <u>veered</u> into the woods, it erupted in a ball of flames.

_____ a. landed

_____ b. turned

_____ c. went straight

_____ Score 3 points for each correct C answer.

_____ Score 2 points for each correct O answer.

_____ **Total Score:** Using Words Precisely

Enter the four total scores in the spaces below, and add them together to find your Reading Comprehension Score. Then record your score on the graph on page 149.

Score	Question Type	Lesson 11
_____	Finding the Main Idea	
_____	Recalling Facts	
_____	Making Inferences	
_____	Using Words Precisely	
_____	**Reading Comprehension Score**	

Author's Approach

Put an X in the box next to the correct answer.

1. The main purpose of the first paragraph is to

☐ a. get the reader's attention.

☐ b. introduce Sandy Purl.

☐ c. convey the mood of the article.

2. Which of the following statements from the article best describes Sandy Purl's attitude towards the passengers on Flight 242?

☐ a. [Purl] knew she needed to calm the passengers.

☐ b. The only thought she had was what she had learned in her safety training: "You are responsible for your passengers."

☐ c. This nurse wanted Purl to go to the hospital with the other survivors, but Purl refused.

3. The authors probably wrote this article in order to

☐ a. describe Sandy Purl's brave actions.

☐ b. inform the reader about the crash of Flight 242.

☐ c. entertain the reader.

_____ Number of correct answers

Record your personal assessment of your work on the Critical Thinking Chart on page 150.

Summarizing and Paraphrasing

Follow the directions provided for questions 1 and 2. Put an X in the box next to the correct answer for question 3.

1. Look for the important ideas and events in paragraphs 11 and 12. Summarize those paragraphs in one or two sentences.

_____

_____

_____

_____

2. Read the statement from the article below. Then read the paraphrase of that statement. Choose the reason that best tells why the paraphrase does not say the same thing as the statement.

   Statement: Purl knew the DC-9 twin engine jet was in trouble.

   Paraphrase: Purl knew that one of the jet's engines was having problems.

   ☐ a. Paraphrase says too much.

   ☐ b. Paraphrase doesn't say enough.

   ☐ c. Paraphrase doesn't agree with the statement from the article.

3. Choose the sentence that correctly restates the following sentence from the article: "As Purl picked through the sheets of hot metal, she enlisted several other surviving passengers to help her."

   ☐ a. Purl found several other passengers who had survived as she searched through the wreckage.

   ☐ b. Purl got several other survivors to help her look through the burnt wreckage.

   ☐ c. As Purl looked through the wreckage, she tried to find passengers who were still alive.

_____ Number of correct answers

Record your personal assessment of your work on the Critical Thinking Chart on page 150.

Critical Thinking

Put an X in the box next to the correct answer for questions 1, 3, and 4. Follow the directions provided for questions 2 and 5.

1. Which of the following statements from the article is an opinion rather than a fact?

   ☐ a. Purl heard three loud bangs in the left engine.

   ☐ b. He aimed the plane for this two-lane highway.

   ☐ c. Purl feared she was trapped.

2. Choose from the letters below to correctly complete the following statement. Write the letters on the lines.

According to paragraph 7, _____ because _____.

   a. the plane's engines malfunctioned

   b. the cabin lights flickered and went out

   c. rain and hail had been sucked into them

3. Into which of the following theme categories would this story fit?

   ☐ a. the dangers of flying

   ☐ b. life is unpredictable

   ☐ c. dedication in the line of duty

4. What was the effect of Flight 242's landing on Route 92?

   ☐ a. Several people were killed.

   ☐ b. The plane's engines were not working.

   ☐ c. It erupted in a ball of flames.

5. Which paragraph(s) provide evidence from the article to

   support your answer to question 4? _____

_____ Number of correct answers

Record your personal assessment of your work on the Critical Thinking Chart on page 150.

Personal Response

I know how Sandy Purl felt because _____

_____

_____

_____

Self-Assessment

What concepts or ideas from the article were difficult?

_____

_____

_____

Which were easy?

_____

_____

_____

Courage at Knifepoint

School bus driver Lilia Rios gets a hug and some roses from one of the students who was on her bus when it was hijacked.

"Take me to Las Vegas!" With these words, a 17-year-old hijacker pressed a knife to Lilia Rios's throat.

2   Lilia Rios had every right to expect a routine day. She drove a bus for the Desert Sands Unified School District in Indio, California. Rios had been driving for 17 years. She had more experience than any of the other drivers.

3   On October 1, 1996, Lilia Rios began her 3 P.M. school bus run. She picked up 90 students at the Roosevelt Elementary School. Her first stop was at King Street and Bliss Avenue. Then she stopped at the corner of Civic Center Drive and Towne Street. After students got off at that stop, only 31 students were still on board. The students were quite young. Most of them were in first or second grade.

4   Just as Rios was about to close the door, a 17-year-old stranger appeared.

He pushed his way onto the bus. Then he pulled out a 12-inch knife. He ordered Rios to drive him to Las Vegas.

5   When Rios hesitated, he hissed, "Lady, do you want me to kill you?" He then added that he would kill the children if she didn't do exactly what he wanted.

6   Rios closed the door of the bus and began to drive. As she did so, she glanced in the rearview mirror. She could see the frightened faces of the young children behind her. Some of them were crying and screaming.

7   Then Rios looked up at the hijacker. "I told myself, 'He's crazy,'" recalled Rios. 'He's going to kill me and the children.'"

8   But Rios was determined not to let that happen. She felt responsible for every single child on her bus. "I love those kids," she said later. "They are like my own."

9   So Rios, a mother of four, formed her own plan. She sensed that the hijacker was nervous. In fact, he seemed just as scared as she was. "I'm not going to listen [to him]," she thought to herself. "I'm not going to play it his way." As they drove, Rios

began talking back to him. When he yelled at her, she yelled back louder. She could see him getting rattled. She could feel herself slowly gaining the upper hand. Still, he kept pressing the blade of his knife against her throat.

10   Meanwhile, the children on the bus continued to scream. One of them was third-grader Laura Campos. At one point Rios passed a bus stop. Campos yelled out the window to people standing there. The people heard Campos's cries and dialed 911. Neither Rios nor the hijacker knew it, but the police would soon be on their way.

11   After several minutes, the hijacker demanded that Rios give him money for gas. She pointed out that it would take a lot of fuel to get all the way to Las Vegas. She told him she didn't have enough money for that. But Rios said she knew where she could get some gas for free. All she had to do was stop at the Desert Sands bus yard. That's where the school buses always filled their tanks. Without giving the hijacker time to say no, Rios turned the bus away from the freeway and headed for the bus yard.

12 When she pulled the bus into the yard, however, the hijacker grew angry. He started screaming. Rios screamed back at him. She stopped the bus, opened the door, and turned to face her captor.

13 Then, suddenly, Rios took a wild chance. She reached out and grabbed at the knife. As she wrestled for control of it, the children in the bus screamed in terror. Rios and the young man tumbled out of the bus. Rios cried out for help. Two mechanics in the yard heard her. "Please help me," she pleaded. "He has a knife. He wants to kill me."

14 The hijacker pulled the knife away from Rios. He scrambled to his feet and ran away.

15 Just then, the police arrived. They caught the hijacker as he fled. The young man was charged with several crimes, including assault with a deadly weapon and kidnapping.

16 For Lilia Rios and the children on the bus, the hijacking had a happy ending. Thanks to Rios, they were all safe. "I'm no hero," said Rios modestly. "I just did my job. The children are fine, and that's what matters. I kept thinking of the kids."

17 Two weeks later, Lilia Rios was honored by other bus drivers and the school district. She was given flowers and a plaque. Third-grader Laura Campos also was honored. It was her screaming out the bus window that brought the police to the scene.

18 Some bus drivers urged Rios to begin driving a different bus route. They thought a change of scenery might help her forget that knife at her throat. But Lilia Rios said no. She wanted to be there for the kids who had also lived through the terror. "When I get on the bus," Lilia Rios said, "I'm going to tell them that I love them." ✺

If you have been timed while reading this article, enter your reading time below. Then turn to the Words-per-Minute Table on page 147 and look up your reading speed (words per minute). Enter your reading speed on the graph on page 148.

Reading Time: Lesson 12

———— : ————
Minutes   Seconds

A Finding the Main Idea

One statement below expresses the main idea of the article. One statement is too general, or too broad. The other statement explains only part of the article; it is too narrow. Label the statements using the following key:

M—Main Idea   **B—Too Broad**   **N—Too Narrow**

_____ 1. Third-grader Laura Campos's screams brought the police to the scene of the kidnapping.

_____ 2. Because of Lilia Rios's brave actions when a 17-year-old with a knife tried to hijack the school bus she was driving, no one was hurt and the hijacker was caught.

_____ 3. Lilia Rios was a bus driver for the Desert Sands Unified School District in California.

_____ Score 15 points for a correct M answer.

_____ Score 5 points for each correct B or N answer.

_____ **Total Score:** Finding the Main Idea

B Recalling Facts

How well do you remember the facts in the article? Put an X in the box next to the answer that correctly completes each statement about the article.

1. When the hijacker boarded Lilia Rios's bus, he ordered her to
   ☐ a. get gas.
   ☐ b. drive to the Desert Sands bus yard.
   ☐ c. drive him to Las Vegas.

2. During the hijacking, Rios was concerned about
   ☐ a. saving her own life.
   ☐ b. the children on the bus.
   ☐ c. cooperating with the hijacker.

3. Rios yelled back at the hijacker when he yelled at her because she
   ☐ a. was afraid.
   ☐ b. wanted to make him more nervous.
   ☐ c. was angry.

4. The police found out about the hijacking because
   ☐ a. one of the students on the bus yelled to people on the street.
   ☐ b. people had witnessed the hijacking.
   ☐ c. mechanics at the Desert Sands bus yard alerted them.

5. When Rios arrived at the Desert Sands bus yard, she
   ☐ a. called the police.
   ☐ b. ran off the bus.
   ☐ c. reached out and grabbed the hijacker's knife.

Score 5 points for each correct answer.

_____ **Total Score:** Recalling Facts

C Making Inferences

When you combine your own experience with information from a text to draw a conclusion that is not directly stated in that text, you are making an inference. Below are five statements that may or may not be inferences based on information in the article. Label the statements using the following key:

C—Correct Inference　　　**F—Faulty Inference**

_____ 1. The 17-year-old hijacker knew Rios.

_____ 2. The children on the bus did not understand what was happening.

_____ 3. The hijacker was not an experienced criminal.

_____ 4. The hijacker didn't really want to kill anyone.

_____ 5. The hijacker wanted money.

Score 5 points for each correct answer.

_____ **Total Score:** Making Inferences

D Using Words Precisely

Each numbered sentence below contains an underlined word or phrase from the article. Following the sentence are three definitions. One definition is closest to the meaning of the underlined word. One definition is opposite or nearly opposite. Label those two definitions using the following key; do not label the remaining definition.

C—Closest　　　**O—Opposite or Nearly Opposite**

1. Lilia Rios had every right to expect a <u>routine</u> day.

_____ a. normal

_____ b. unusual

_____ c. frightening

2. When Rios <u>hesitated</u>, he hissed, "Lady, do you want me to kill you?"

_____ a. continued

_____ b. froze

_____ c. paused

3. She <u>sensed</u> that the hijacker was nervous.

_____ a. didn't realize

_____ b. felt

_____ c. knew

4. She could see him getting <u>rattled</u>.

_____ a. angry

_____ b. calm

_____ c. upset

5. The young man was charged with several crimes, including <u>assault</u> with a deadly weapon and kidnapping.

_____ a. attack

_____ b. threat

_____ c. help

_____ Score 3 points for each correct C answer.

_____ Score 2 points for each correct O answer.

_____ **Total Score:** Using Words Precisely

Enter the four total scores in the spaces below, and add them together to find your Reading Comprehension Score. Then record your score on the graph on page 149.

Score	Question Type	Lesson 12
_____	Finding the Main Idea	
_____	Recalling Facts	
_____	Making Inferences	
_____	Using Words Precisely	
_____	**Reading Comprehension Score**	

Author's Approach

Put an X in the box next to the correct answer.

1. What do the authors mean by the statement, "Lilia Rios had every right to expect a routine day"?

☐ a. Lilia Rios did not deserve what happened to her.

☐ b. On the day of the hijacking, there was no reason for Lilia Rios to suspect her day would be different from any other.

☐ c. Since she was an experienced driver, Lilia Rios should have had no trouble handling a hijacker.

2. What is the authors' purpose in writing, "Courage at Knifepoint"?

☐ a. to inform the reader about Lilia Rios's bravery

☐ b. to express an opinion about Lilia Rios

☐ c. to entertain the reader

3. The authors tell this story mainly by

☐ a. sharing different points of view.

☐ b. retelling Lilia Rios's personal experiences.

☐ c. telling different stories about the same topic.

_____ Number of correct answers

Record your personal assessment of your work on the Critical Thinking Chart on page 150.

Summarizing and Paraphrasing

Follow the directions provided for the following questions.

1. Look for the important ideas and events in paragraphs 9 and 10. Summarize those paragraphs in one or two sentences.

_____

_____

_____

_____

2. Reread paragraph 13 in the article. Below, write a summary of the paragraph in no more than 25 words.

_____

_____

_____

_____

Reread your summary and decide whether it covers the important ideas in the paragraph. Next, decide how to shorten the summary to 15 words or less without leaving out any essential information. Write this summary below.

_____

_____

_____

_____

3. Read the statement from the article below. Then read the paraphrase of that statement. Choose the reason that best tells why the paraphrase does not say the same thing as the statement.

Statement: But Rios was determined not to let that happen.

Paraphrase: Rios thought that would not happen.

☐ a. Paraphrase says too much.

☐ b. Paraphrase doesn't say enough.

☐ c. Paraphrase doesn't agree with the statement from the article.

_____ Number of correct answers

Record your personal assessment of your work on the Critical Thinking Chart on page 150.

Critical Thinking

Follow the directions provided for questions 1, 2, and 3. Put an X in the box next to the correct answer for question 4.

1. For each statement below, write *O* if it expresses an opinion or *F* if it expresses a fact.

_____ a. He seemed just as scared as she was.

_____ b. Rios said she knew where she could get some free gas.

_____ c. They thought a change of scenery might help her forget that knife at her throat.

2. Which paragraph(s) provide evidence from the article to support your answers to question 1? _____

3. Choose from the letters below to correctly complete the following statement. Write the letters on the lines.

According to paragraph 18, _____ because _____.

   a.   her screams had brought the police to the scene of the hijacking

   b.   Lilia Rios was honored

   c.   Laura Campos was honored

4. What was the effect of Lilia Rios's yelling back at the hijacker?

☐ a. He held a knife against her throat.

☐ b. He got more upset.

☐ c. She didn't listen to him.

_____ Number of correct answers

Record your personal assessment of your work on the Critical Thinking Chart on page 150.

Personal Response

If I had been on Lilia Rios's bus I would have _____

_____

_____

_____

_____

Self-Assessment

While reading the article, I was having trouble with _____

_____

_____

_____

_____

Rescue Mission

U.S. Marines on duty in Vietnam

"Get us out of here!" pleaded a voice on the radio. "For God's sake, get us out!" The call came from the leader of 12 American soldiers trapped inside Cambodia. These soldiers were in big trouble. A large force of enemy troops had surrounded them. Four of the soldiers were already dead. All of the remaining eight were wounded.

2   It was May 2, 1968. America was at war in Vietnam. Cambodia was not part of the war. But enemy troops from North Vietnam often traveled through Cambodia. So U.S. troops sometimes went there, too, in order

to spy on the enemy. That's what the 12 Americans had been doing. But 30 miles inside Cambodia, they had been trapped. Could anyone save them?

3 Sergeant Roy Benavidez was at Loc Ninh in Vietnam when the distress call came in. He could hear the sound of gunfire over the airwaves. "There was so much shooting," he said, "it sounded like a popcorn machine."

4 Three helicopters were sent to rescue the stranded men. But the choppers couldn't land. The enemy blasted them every time they came close. At last, the pilots flew back to Loc Ninh. Benavidez ran to the first chopper. A wounded crewman fell out and landed in his arms. A few moments later, the man died.

5 Soon another chopper was sent to try to rescue the Americans. Benavidez grabbed his rifle and climbed on board. No one ordered him to go. But he knew his fellow soldiers were in trouble. He wanted to help. He later said, "When I got on that 'copter, little did I know we were going to spend six hours in hell."

6 When this helicopter neared the trouble spot, the enemy was still firing away. It was impossible to get near the wounded men. The pilot flew to within 75 yards. But he could not get any closer than that. With the chopper hovering 10 feet off the ground, Benavidez made his move. He jumped out onto the ground. Then, all alone, he dashed through a field toward the wounded men.

7 Enemy soldiers saw him. They opened fire. Bullets flew all around him. They hit him in the head, the face, and the right leg. Several times Benavidez fell down. But each time he scrambled to his feet and kept running. "When you're shot," he said, "you feel a burning pain like you've been touched with a hot metal. The fear that you experience is worse—and that's what keeps you going."

8 At last Benavidez reached the stranded troops. He used a smoke grenade to mark a place where the chopper could land. Then he turned to the wounded men. He told them they had to shoot back at the enemy as hard and fast as they could. That would distract the enemy long enough to let the helicopter fly in.

9 The plan worked. With the Americans training their fire on the enemy, the pilot managed to get to the spot Benavidez had marked. Then Benavidez picked up one of the wounded men. Ignoring the pain of his own wounds, he carried the man to the chopper. Then he ran back for the next man. He managed to get four of the wounded men on board.

Sergeant Roy Benavidez

10   But before Benavidez could do anything more, he was hit in the back and stomach. He fell to the ground. As he looked up, he saw the helicopter get hit, too. It burst into flames. Benavidez struggled to his feet. He raced to the wreck. The pilot and two of the wounded soldiers were dead. Benavidez pulled the other men out of the fire. He gathered them into a circle with the four other wounded soldiers. The situation looked hopeless. It seemed the enemy could overrun them at any time.

11   Benavidez used his radio to call for help. Soon helicopters arrived and began shooting at the enemy. Benavidez kept his little group firing away too. Meanwhile, he did his best to treat the men's wounds. He also tried to care for his own wounds. Still, blood from his head trickled into his eyes. That made it hard for him to see. As he tended to one of his men, a bullet struck him in the thigh. It was another of the 36 wounds that Roy Benavidez would suffer before the day was over.

12   More choppers came to get the men out. But enemy fire knocked most of them out of the sky. At last, after several hours, one got close enough to land. Once more, Benavidez began to drag wounded soldiers to the chopper. But his ordeal was not over yet.

13   As he went to pick up one man, an enemy soldier charged at him. The enemy hit him over the head with the butt of a rifle. Benavidez wheeled around. He saw that the soldier was about to stab him with his bayonet. Desperately, Benavidez reached for the blade. As he grabbed it, the bayonet cut through his hand. But at least that stopped the thrust. Then Benavidez took out his own knife and killed the soldier.

14   Benavidez stumbled back to the helicopter. He was bleeding heavily from his many wounds. Yet he helped load the rest of the wounded men onto the chopper. He even shot down two more enemy soldiers as they charged toward him.

15   At last, when all the other men were on board, Benavidez allowed himself to be pulled into the chopper. He collapsed on the floor. His intestines were spilling out of a wound in his stomach. He had to use his hands to hold them in.

16   With enemy bullets still flying, the chopper took off. Luckily, the bullets did not hit anything vital. The group made it back to Loc Ninh safely.

17   By then, Benavidez had lost a huge amount of blood. He had no strength left. He could not move or speak. The first doctor who looked at him thought he was dead. To show he was not, Benavidez did the only thing he could manage. He spit in the doctor's face.

18   It took Benavidez a long time to recover from his wounds. His actions won him the nation's highest medal. This was the Congressional Medal of Honor. His award read in part, "For conspicuous gallantry . . . above and beyond the call of duty."

19   A Mexican American, Benavidez felt a great sense of loyalty towards the United States. "I'm proud to be an American," he said. "I'm proud to serve my country—serve it well. I'm proud of being rewarded for a job well done."

20   Still, Benavidez did not think of himself as a hero. Once someone told him that his one-man battle was extraordinary. "No," replied Roy Benavidez. "That's duty."

If you have been timed while reading this article, enter your reading time below. Then turn to the Words-per-Minute Table on page 147 and look up your reading speed (words per minute). Enter your reading speed on the graph on page 148.

Reading Time: Lesson 13

———— : ————
Minutes   Seconds

A | Finding the Main Idea

One statement below expresses the main idea of the article. One statement is too general, or too broad. The other statement explains only part of the article; it is too narrow. Label the statements using the following key:

M—Main Idea   **B—Too Broad**   **N—Too Narrow**

_____ 1. Sergeant Roy Benavidez risked his life in an effort to save eight American soldiers trapped in Cambodia.

_____ 2. Sergeant Roy Benavidez saved many lives while serving as a soldier in the Vietnam War.

_____ 3. Sergeant Roy Benavidez was wounded 36 times during a rescue mission in Cambodia.

_____ Score 15 points for a correct M answer.

_____ Score 5 points for each correct B or N answer.

_____ **Total Score:** Finding the Main Idea

B | Recalling Facts

How well do you remember the facts in the article? Put an X in the box next to the answer that correctly completes each statement about the article.

1. The first group of helicopters sent to rescue the trapped soldiers
   ☐ a. couldn't land because they were being shot at.
   ☐ b. were shot down.
   ☐ c. rescued some of the men.

2. Benavidez climbed on one of the helicopters because he
   ☐ a. was ordered to.
   ☐ b. knew the stranded soldiers.
   ☐ c. wanted to help.

3. The first helicopter that landed near the wounded men
   ☐ a. carried four of them to safety.
   ☐ b. was shot and burst into flames.
   ☐ c. carried Benavidez and the other wounded men back to Loc Ninh.

4. Benavidez spit in the doctor's face because
   ☐ a. he was in pain.
   ☐ b. he was too weak to do anything else.
   ☐ c. he didn't like the doctor.

5. Benavidez received the Congressional Medal of Honor for
   ☐ a. doing more than was expected of him.
   ☐ b. doing his duty.
   ☐ c. being injured in battle.

Score 5 points for each correct answer.

_____ **Total Score:** Recalling Facts

C   Making Inferences

When you combine your own experience with information from a text to draw a conclusion that is not directly stated in that text, you are making an inference. Below are five statements that may or may not be inferences based on information in the article. Label the statements using the following key:

C—Correct Inference   **F—Faulty Inference**

_____   1. Cambodia is near Vietnam.

_____   2. The enemy soldiers wanted to take the American soldiers prisoner.

_____   3. Roy Benavidez was the only soldier who wanted to help the trapped soldiers.

_____   4. The bullets that hit Benavidez did not strike any important organs.

_____   5. Benavidez was born in Mexico.

Score 5 points for each correct answer.

_____ **Total Score:** Making Inferences

D   Using Words Precisely

Each numbered sentence below contains an underlined word or phrase from the article. Following the sentence are three definitions. One definition is closest to the meaning of the underlined word. One definition is opposite or nearly opposite. Label those two definitions using the following key; do not label the remaining definition.

C—Closest   **O—Opposite or Nearly Opposite**

1. With the chopper <u>hovering</u> 10 feet off the ground, Benavidez made his move.

_____   a. hanging

_____   b. moving forward

_____   c. landing

2. That would <u>distract</u> the enemy long enough to let the helicopter fly in.

_____   a. focus

_____   b. frighten

_____   c. draw away

3. But his <u>ordeal</u> was not over yet.

_____   a. experience

_____   b. pleasure

_____   c. suffering

4. Luckily, the bullets did not hit anything <u>vital</u>.

_____   a. important

_____   b. living

_____   c. useless

5. Once someone told him that his one-man battle was <u>extraordinary.</u>

_____ a. brave

_____ b. remarkable

_____ c. ordinary

_____ Score 3 points for each correct C answer.

_____ Score 2 points for each correct O answer.

_____ **Total Score:** Using Words Precisely

Enter the four total scores in the spaces below, and add them together to find your Reading Comprehension Score. Then record your score on the graph on page 149.

Score	Question Type	Lesson 13
_____	Finding the Main Idea	
_____	Recalling Facts	
_____	Making Inferences	
_____	Using Words Precisely	
_____	**Reading Comprehension Score**	

Author's Approach

Put an X in the box next to the correct answer.

1. The main purpose of the first paragraph is to

☐ a. give background information for the story.

☐ b. entertain the reader.

☐ c. introduce Roy Benavidez.

2. What is the authors' purpose in writing "Rescue Mission"?

☐ a. to inform the reader about the Vietnam War

☐ b. to express an opinion about American soldiers

☐ c. to describe Roy Benavidez's brave rescue

3. In this article, "No one ordered [Benavidez] to go" means

☐ a. Benavidez was not supposed to go on the rescue mission.

☐ b. Benavidez went on the dangerous mission because he wanted to, not because he had to.

☐ c. no one knew why Benavidez went on the rescue mission.

_____ Number of correct answers

Record your personal assessment of your work on the Critical Thinking Chart on page 150.

Summarizing and Paraphrasing

Follow the directions provided for questions 1 and 2. Put an X in the box next to the correct answer for question 3.

1. Look for the important ideas and events in paragraphs 7 and 8. Summarize those paragraphs in one or two sentences.

_____

_____

_____

_____

2. Complete the following one-sentence summary of the article using the lettered phrases from the phrase bank below. Write the letters on the lines.

> **Phrase Bank**
> a. how he rescued the soldiers
> b. the situation he went into
> c. a description of his feelings about his actions

The article about Roy Benavidez begins with _____, goes on to explain _____, and ends with _____.

3. Choose the best one-sentence paraphrase for the following sentence from the article: " 'When I got on that 'copter, little did I know we were going to spend six hours in hell.' "

☐ a. When I got on that helicopter, I didn't know what would happen.

☐ b. When I got on that helicopter, I didn't know where we were going.

☐ c. When I got on that helicopter, I didn't know how bad it would be.

_____ Number of correct answers

Record your personal assessment of your work on the Critical Thinking Chart on page 150.

Critical Thinking

Put an X in the box next to the correct answer for questions 1, 3, 4, and 5. Follow the directions provided for question 2.

1. Which of the following statements from the article is an opinion rather than a fact?

☐ a. [Benavidez] could hear the sound of gunfire over the airwaves.

☐ b. It seemed the enemy could overrun them at any time.

☐ c. Benavidez stumbled back to the helicopter.

2. Choose from the letters below to correctly complete the following statement. Write the letters on the lines.

According to paragraph 2, _____ because _____.

   a.   they wanted to spy on Vietnamese troops

   b.   they were trapped

   c.   U.S. troops were in Cambodia

3. What did you have to do to answer question 2?

☐ a. find a description (how something looks)

☐ b. find an effect (something that happened)

☐ c. find a purpose (why something is done)

4. What was the effect of Benavidez grabbing an enemy soldier's bayonet?

☐ a. Benavidez killed the soldier.

☐ b. The bayonet cut through his hand.

☐ c. Benavidez was hit over the head.

5. Into which of the following theme categories would this story best fit?

☐ a. battles of the Vietnam War

☐ b. prisoners of war

☐ c. beyond the call of duty

_____ Number of correct answers

Record your personal assessment of your work on the Critical Thinking Chart on page 150.

Personal Response

What was most surprising or interesting to you about this article?

_____

_____

_____

_____

Self-Assessment

I can't really understand how _____

_____

_____

_____

Fallen Heroes

Firefighters stand at the scene as the Worcester Cold Storage and Warehouse continues to burn. Six firefighters died in the blaze.

It was just an empty building. The 80-year-old warehouse in the city of Worcester, Massachusetts had not been used for a long time. But the building's five floors were not always deserted. Homeless people who had no other place to stay often slipped into the warehouse to get out of the cold. Sometimes these people stayed all night.

2   That was the case on December 3, 1999. A man and a woman were staying on the second floor of the warehouse. In fact, they had been living there for months. On this

night, though, the couple apparently had a fight. Police believe they accidentally tipped over a lighted candle. The flame spread to some clothes and papers. The couple tried to put out the growing fire. When they couldn't, they panicked and ran away. They did not ring any fire alarms. And they told no one that the building was now empty.

3   Worcester firefighters were called to the blaze just after six o'clock in the evening. About 25 of them went into the warehouse. They went in to fight the fire. But they were also looking to see if anyone was inside. The firefighters knew that homeless people used the warehouse as a shelter. They wanted to save anyone who might be trapped there.

4   When they got inside, they found the second, third, and fourth floors engulfed in flames. Still, the fire looked manageable at first. Then, without warning, it flared up. The heat, smoke, and flames were so fearsome that Fire Chief Michael McNamee called for extra help.

5   Ten more firefighters came to the warehouse. By then the fire had grown even worse. The old brick warehouse was a firetrap. It was a maze of dark, smoky rooms. None of these rooms had windows. The lack of windows meant that the fire's heat was trapped inside. Large areas of open space helped to spread the fire. Also, the ceiling and walls had cork insulation. The burning cork added to the smoke. "You couldn't see six inches in front of your face," said McNamee.

6   All fires are hard to fight. But a fire in an abandoned building is especially difficult. That is because such buildings are often in bad shape. People come in and rip out the plumbing and wiring. They sell the materials for scrap. But that leaves holes in the floors and walls. Sometimes steps in the stairways are missing. Walking through such a place can be very dangerous. The firefighters had to walk through it in the dark while almost blind from the smoke. They knew they were risking their lives with every step they took.

7   Soon Fire Chief McNamee realized that his firefighters faced a nearly hopeless task. The fire was out of control. So he told everyone to get out of the building. Then he ordered a head count. By then it was about 7:30 P.M. McNamee wanted to make sure all his people were out. But they weren't. Two men—Paul Brotherton and Jerry Lucey—were missing.

8   Just then, McNamee received an urgent radio message. It came from Brotherton. He and Lucey were still inside the warehouse. "Mayday! Mayday!" cried Brotherton. "We're running out of air."

9   McNamee asked where they were. Brotherton said they were on the third floor. There was no way the Worcester crew would just leave them there to die. The other firefighters had to try to rescue them. So McNamee quickly put together several two-person search teams. These teams headed into the building to find Brotherton and Lucey. By this time the smoke was so thick the teams had to use guide ropes to find their way back outside again.

10   "We kept sweeping and sweeping and sweeping and we still couldn't find them," recalled McNamee. "It's like being in a maze. Zero visibility. High heat. Fire. That's what [the search teams] were facing." At last, McNamee told the teams to get out.

He didn't want to lose any more people.

11 But the nightmare was getting worse. Four men from the search teams couldn't make it out of the building. They were Timothy Jackson, James Lyons, Joseph McGuirk, and Thomas Spencer. So now a total of six men were trapped inside the flaming warehouse. A sickening feeling settled over the other firefighters. They knew their comrades were dying inside the building. But there was nothing more they could do.

12 News of the fire had spread quickly. Hundreds of firefighters from nearby towns arrived on the scene. But they, too, were helpless to save the six men. Firefighters kept dousing the warehouse with water. But the fire had eaten through the entire building. Soon all the floors collapsed onto each other.

13 All night the fire raged. The next morning, smoke and flames were still leaping into the air. At last, in the middle of the day, the flames finally began to die down. Only then could firefighters get inside the ruined building. They were able to recover the body of Timothy Jackson. But the wreckage of the building was so great that it took a week to find all the other bodies.

14 The tragic death of the six firefighters stunned the city of Worcester. The day after the men died, Mayor Raymond Mariano said, "This morning the sun didn't rise. It didn't rise because last night we lost six members of our family."

15 The fallen men left behind five widows and 17 children. Sympathy and money poured in for them. People were especially touched to learn about *The Fireman's Prayer*. This prayer hung in the home that Paul Brotherton had shared with his wife and six sons. The prayer read, "When I am called to duty, God, wherever flames may rage, give me strength to save some life. And if according to your will I have to lose my life, please bless with your protecting hand my children and my wife."

16 Mourning for the dead men spread beyond the city of Worcester. The rest of the nation also felt the loss. It was the highest U.S. firefighter death toll in a burning building in more than 20 years. In fact, firefighters around the world grieved for the fallen men. More than 30,000 came to Worcester to honor them. Firefighters came from as far away as Ireland and Australia. As one New Jersey firefighter said, "We came to show we care."

17 The six Worcester firefighters were true heroes. Mayor Mariano put it this way: "Heroes are not individuals who bounce basketballs or hit baseballs in front of thousands of screaming fans. . . . Heroes are average men and women who reach out unselfishly to help those in need."

A | Finding the Main Idea

One statement below expresses the main idea of the article. One statement is too general, or too broad. The other statement explains only part of the article; it is too narrow. Label the statements using the following key:

M—Main Idea   **B—Too Broad**   **N—Too Narrow**

_____ 1. In Worcester, Massachusetts, six firefighters lost their lives when they went into a burning warehouse to rescue anyone who was inside.

_____ 2. Police believe that homeless people caused the fire in the Worcester warehouse by tipping over a candle.

_____ 3. A fire in Worcester, Massachusetts, in 1999 killed six firefighters.

_____ Score 15 points for a correct M answer.

_____ Score 5 points for each correct B or N answer.

_____ **Total Score:** Finding the Main Idea

B | Recalling Facts

How well do you remember the facts in the article? Put an X in the box next to the answer that correctly completes each statement about the article.

1. The people who started the fire in the empty warehouse
   ☐ a. were homeless people who had been living there.
   ☐ b. called the fire department to report it.
   ☐ c. were some of the many homeless people in the building at the time.

2. When the firefighters first went into the warehouse,
   ☐ a. the fire flared up.
   ☐ b. they found some homeless people.
   ☐ c. they thought the fire looked manageable.

3. The fire spread quickly because
   ☐ a. the warehouse had dark, smoky rooms.
   ☐ b. there were large areas of open space.
   ☐ c. the ceiling and walls had cork insulation.

4. When the fire chief realized that two of the firefighters were trapped inside, he sent
   ☐ a. an urgent radio message.
   ☐ b. four firefighters in after them.
   ☐ c. several two-person search teams in after them.

5. The loss of the six firefighters
   ☐ a. was the highest ever in a fire in the United States.
   ☐ b. was the highest death toll from a building fire in the United States in 20 years.
   ☐ c. went unnoticed.

Score 5 points for each correct answer.

_____ **Total Score:** Recalling Facts

C Making Inferences

When you combine your own experience with information from a text to draw a conclusion that is not directly stated in that text, you are making an inference. Below are five statements that may or may not be inferences based on information in the article. Label the statements using the following key:

C—Correct Inference   **F—Faulty Inference**

_____ 1. The empty warehouse in Worcester was about to be torn down.

_____ 2. The city of Worcester did not know that homeless people sometimes stayed in the warehouse.

_____ 3. The firefighters would not have been killed if they had not gone in to look for people in the warehouse.

_____ 4. Firefighters Paul Brotherton and Jerry Lucey couldn't find their way out of the building.

_____ 5. Firefighters usually work in pairs.

Score 5 points for each correct answer.

_____ **Total Score:** Making Inferences

D Using Words Precisely

Each numbered sentence below contains an underlined word or phrase from the article. Following the sentence are three definitions. One definition is closest to the meaning of the underlined word. One definition is opposite or nearly opposite. Label those two definitions using the following key; do not label the remaining definition.

C—Closest   **O—Opposite or Nearly Opposite**

1. But a fire in an <u>abandoned</u> building is especially difficult.

_____ a. empty

_____ b. run-down

_____ c. used

2. Just then, McNamee received an <u>urgent</u> radio message.

_____ a. frightened

_____ b. unimportant

_____ c. very important

3. People were especially <u>touched</u> to learn about *The Fireman's Prayer.*

_____ a. surprised

_____ b. moved

_____ c. unimpressed

4. In fact, firefighters around the world <u>grieved for</u> the fallen men.

_____ a. were sad for

_____ b. cheered for

_____ c. heard about

5. "Heroes are <u>average</u> men and women who reach out unselfishly to help those in need."

_____ a. dedicated

_____ b. outstanding

_____ c. ordinary

_____ Score 3 points for each correct C answer.

_____ Score 2 points for each correct O answer.

_____ **Total Score:** Using Words Precisely

Enter the four total scores in the spaces below, and add them together to find your Reading Comprehension Score. Then record your score on the graph on page 149.

Score	Question Type	Lesson 14
_____	Finding the Main Idea	
_____	Recalling Facts	
_____	Making Inferences	
_____	Using Words Precisely	
_____	**Reading Comprehension Score**	

Author's Approach

Put an X in the box next to the correct answer.

1. The main purpose of the first paragraph is to

☐ a. inform the reader about the empty warehouse in Worcester, Massachusetts.

☐ b. give background information for the story.

☐ c. express an opinion about the people who stayed in the old warehouse.

2. What do the authors mean by the statement, "And [the homeless couple] told no one that the building was now empty"?

☐ a. If the homeless couple had told the fire department that the building was empty, the six firefighters might not have died.

☐ b. The homeless couple should have checked to see if the building was empty before leaving.

☐ c. The homeless couple did not see anyone as they were leaving the building.

3. The authors tell this story mainly by

☐ a. retelling the personal experiences of the trapped firefighters.

☐ b. comparing the Worcester fire with other fires.

☐ c. telling the story from different people's points of view.

_____ Number of correct answers

Record your personal assessment of your work on the Critical Thinking Chart on page 150.

Summarizing and Paraphrasing

Follow the directions provided for questions 1 and 2. Put an X in the box next to the correct answer for question 3.

1. Reread paragraph 6 in the article. Below, write a summary of the paragraph in no more than 25 words.

_____

_____

_____

Reread your summary and decide whether it covers the important ideas in the paragraph. Next, decide how to shorten the summary to 15 words or less without leaving out any essential information. Write this summary below.

_____

_____

_____

2. Read the statement from the article below. Then read the paraphrase of that statement. Choose the reason that best tells why the paraphrase does not say the same thing as the statement.

Statement: They knew they were risking their lives with every step they took.

Paraphrase: They knew it was dangerous walking down the stairs.

☐ a. Paraphrase says too much.

☐ b. Paraphrase doesn't say enough.

☐ c. Paraphrase doesn't agree with the statement from the article.

3. Choose the sentence that correctly restates the following sentence from the article: "Large areas of open space helped to spread the fire."

☐ a. There was a lot of empty space in the warehouse.

☐ b. The fire spread more quickly because there was so much open space in the warehouse.

☐ c. The fire spread through the open spaces in the building.

_____ Number of correct answers

Record your personal assessment of your work on the Critical Thinking Chart on page 150.

Critical Thinking

Follow the directions provided for questions 1, 2, and 4. Put an X in the box next to the correct answer for questions 3 and 5.

1. For each statement below, write O if it expresses an opinion or F if it expresses a fact.

_____ a. Police believe they accidentally tipped over a lighted candle.

_____ b. Still, the fire looked manageable at first.

_____ c. At last, in the middle of the day, the flames finally began to die down.

2. Choose from the letters below to correctly complete the following statement. Write the letters on the lines.

    According to paragraph 9, _____ because _____.

    a. two firefighters were trapped inside

    b. the fire chief sent search teams into the burning warehouse

    c. they had to use ropes to find their way out

3. What was the effect of sending search teams into the building to find Brotherton and Lucey?

    ☐ a. The fire was out of control.

    ☐ b. Brotherton and Lucey died in the building.

    ☐ c. Four more men were lost.

4. Which paragraph(s) provide evidence from the article to support your answer to question 3? _____

5. If you were a fire chief, how would you use the information in the article to train new recruits?

    ☐ a. to demonstrate why they should not try to save the people in burning buildings

    ☐ b. to illustrate the dedication firefighters should have

    ☐ c. to show the results of underestimating a fire

_____ Number of correct answers

Record your personal assessment of your work on the Critical Thinking Chart on page 150.

Personal Response

What would you have done if you were the fire chief who discovered that two of your men were missing?

_____

_____

_____

_____

Self-Assessment

A word or phrase in the article that I do not understand is _____

_____

_____

_____

Terror at the YMCA

Rescue workers at the scene at the West Roxbury, Massachusetts, YMCA shortly after the ceiling collapsed

David Bortolotto thought he heard a loud crack. He looked up at the ceiling, but it looked fine. So he went back to work.

2   Bortolotto was a lifeguard at the YMCA pool in West Roxbury, Massachusetts. At 2 P.M. on September 18, 1989, he was in the shallow end of the 55-foot swimming pool. He was teaching nine young children how to swim. These children ranged in age from 3 to 6.

3   Some of the children's parents were watching from the waiting room. They could see the pool through a glass window. Ellenmarie Joyce could see them too. Joyce was the director of swim classes. She was in her office near the pool.

4   Suddenly, Bortolotto heard a second loud crack. This time when he looked up, he saw a piece of concrete falling from the ceiling. It was headed straight at him and the kids. Quickly, the 18-year-old Bortolotto grabbed a child who was standing on the pool deck just in front of him. He pulled the child toward him into the water. As he did, he shielded the child with his own body.

5   A piece of the roof hit Bortolotto on the head. It opened up a 12-inch gash in his head and took off a chunk of his skin. Blood started to pour out. Yet Bortolotto barely noticed this. His heart was racing too fast to feel the pain. His only concern was for the kids in the water. More of the roof was now falling. Concrete, tar, and roofing came tumbling down. Bortolotto swam through the debris to guide four children out of the pool. A huge 20-by-15 foot hole had opened up in the roof. Anyone looking up could see the sky.

6   Joyce, also a trained lifeguard, didn't see the roof collapse. But she heard enough to know there was trouble in the pool. First, she heard the loud bang. Then the laughter and giggles of the children turned into shrill cries of horror. Joyce rushed out of her office to see what was wrong.

7   "I just saw David," said Joyce, who had hired Bortolotto only two weeks before. "I saw a foot and I saw him looking around, and I just went in." As she dove into the water, Joyce wasn't thinking about her own safety. She was focused only on saving the children. "The three closest to me I just grabbed," she said.

8   Joyce didn't know how many children were in the class. She wasn't sure they were all safe. So she kept diving under the water to look for more.

9   Some of the parents in the waiting room saw the ceiling give way. One said she saw what looked like bits of confetti falling. But it wasn't confetti. What she saw were really bits of ceiling tiles. A second or two later, the roof caved in. The parents ran to the door that led to the pool deck. But the door was locked from the outside. They had to run through the locker room to reach the pool.

10   William Scafani, director of the West Roxbury YMCA, was also in the water at the time. When the ceiling collapsed, he, too, thought of the children. Scafani motioned to a man named William McDonald,

who happened to be at the edge of the pool. McDonald had come to the pool for a swim. Instead, Scafani was asking him to help look for injured children.

11   Scafani and McDonald quickly swam to the shallow end. By then, a lot of debris had fallen into the water. The men couldn't tell if a child was trapped underneath the debris. So again and again they dove under to look.

12   "It was total bedlam," said McDonald later. "Kids were crying and parents [were] screaming. I thought, 'My God, [children] must be trapped [under the debris].' So I jumped in and looked for bodies. We just kept searching until we were sure they were all out."

13   Bortolotto knew the size of his class. So he did a quick head count. That proved that all the children were out of the pool. Two of the kids, it seems, had gotten out on their own.

14   It was a good thing the adults acted so fast. A few moments after everyone was out of the pool, a second section of the roof came crashing down. Luckily, no one was hurt by this incident.

15   Still, enough harm had been done by the first collapse. Seven of the children had been hit by falling debris. Two of them were badly injured. They had fractured skulls.

16   The good news was that no one died. But Bortolotto had come very close. The piece of concrete that hit him nearly killed him. He needed 100 stitches to close the gash. If the concrete had fallen one inch farther to the right, it would have struck him in the middle of his head.

17   At first, Bortolotto had no idea how badly hurt he was. When he was under the water looking for kids, he knew he had gotten hit. It was only after everyone was safely out of the pool that Joyce saw his bleeding head. She said, "You look hurt."

18   "My head sort of hurts," Bortolotto said. He was then placed on a stretcher and rushed to the hospital.

19   Everyone agreed that Bortolotto and Joyce deserved a lot of credit. Both had risked their lives to make sure no child died. "This could have been much, much worse," said Gerard McHale of the Boston Police. "We owe thanks to a young man and woman who were real American heroes."

If you have been timed while reading this article, enter your reading time below. Then turn to the Words-per-Minute Table on page 147 and look up your reading speed (words per minute). Enter your reading speed on the graph on page 148.

Reading Time: Lesson 15

_____ : _____

Minutes   Seconds

A | Finding the Main Idea

One statement below expresses the main idea of the article. One statement is too general, or too broad. The other statement explains only part of the article; it is too narrow. Label the statements using the following key:

M—Main Idea   **B—Too Broad**   **N—Too Narrow**

_____ 1. When the roof over the pool at a YMCA in Massachusetts collapsed, several employees risked their lives to make sure all the children in the water were safe.

_____ 2. A piece of the falling roof hit lifeguard David Bortolotto in the head, opening up a 12-inch gash in his head.

_____ 3. The roof over the pool in a YMCA in Massachusetts collapsed.

_____ Score 15 points for a correct M answer.

_____ Score 5 points for each correct B or N answer.

_____ **Total Score:** Finding the Main Idea

B | Recalling Facts

How well do you remember the facts in the article? Put an X in the box next to the answer that correctly completes each statement about the article.

1. When Bortolotto heard the first loud crack,
☐ a. he quickly got out of the pool.
☐ b. he kept working.
☐ c. a large piece of concrete started falling toward him.

2. Ellenmarie Joyce left her office because she
☐ a. had seen the roof collapse.
☐ b. heard a loud bang and screams.
☐ c. saw David Bortolotto.

3. When the director of the YMCA saw the ceiling collapse, he
☐ a. asked another man to help him look for trapped children.
☐ b. jumped into the water to help the children.
☐ c. ran out of his office to the pool.

4. When the second section of roof fell,
☐ a. it hit seven of the children.
☐ b. Bortolotto was nearly killed.
☐ c. everyone was already out of the pool.

5. The piece of concrete that hit Bortolotto
☐ a. nearly killed him.
☐ b. fractured his skull.
☐ c. struck him in the middle of the head.

Score 5 points for each correct answer.

_____ **Total Score:** Recalling Facts

C Making Inferences

When you combine your own experience with information from a text to draw a conclusion that is not directly stated in that text, you are making an inference. Below are five statements that may or may not be inferences based on information in the article. Label the statements using the following key:

C—Correct Inference   **F—Faulty Inference**

_____ 1. The ceiling of the YMCA building was poorly constructed.

_____ 2. Bortolotto had been trained on how to save lives.

_____ 3. The cut in Bortolotto's head was not very painful.

_____ 4. The children in the pool did not know how to swim.

_____ 5. There was open swimming at the time that the ceiling collapsed.

Score 5 points for each correct answer.

_____ **Total Score:** Making Inferences

D Using Words Precisely

Each numbered sentence below contains an underlined word or phrase from the article. Following the sentence are three definitions. One definition is closest to the meaning of the underlined word. One definition is opposite or nearly opposite. Label those two definitions using the following key; do not label the remaining definition.

C—Closest   **O—Opposite or Nearly Opposite**

1. He was in the <u>shallow</u> end of the 55-foot swimming pool.

_____ a. deep

_____ b. far

_____ c. low

2. As he did, he <u>shielded</u> the child with his own body.

_____ a. carried

_____ b. protected

_____ c. exposed

3. Then the laughter and giggles of the children turned into <u>shrill</u> cries of horror.

_____ a. sharp

_____ b. soft

_____ c. loud

4. When the ceiling <u>collapsed</u>, he, too, thought of the children.

_____ a. was put up

_____ b. fell in

_____ c. broke

5. "It was total <u>bedlam</u>," said McDonald later.

_____ a. confusion

_____ b. sleeplessness

_____ c. calm

_____ Score 3 points for each correct C answer.

_____ Score 2 points for each correct O answer.

_____ **Total Score:** Using Words Precisely

Enter the four total scores in the spaces below, and add them together to find your Reading Comprehension Score. Then record your score on the graph on page 149.

Score	Question Type	Lesson 15
_____	Finding the Main Idea	
_____	Recalling Facts	
_____	Making Inferences	
_____	Using Words Precisely	
_____	**Reading Comprehension Score**	

Author's Approach

Put an X in the box next to the correct answer.

1. The authors use the first sentence of the article to

☐ a. entertain the reader.

☐ b. get the reader's attention.

☐ c. describe David Bortolotto.

2. What is the authors' purpose in writing "Terror at the YMCA"?

☐ a. to describe what happened when the roof collapsed

☐ b. to express an opinion about David Bortolotto and Ellenmarie Joyce

☐ c. to persuade the reader not to swim at the YMCA

3. From the statements below, choose the one that you believe the authors would agree with.

☐ a. Joyce did not trust Bortolotto.

☐ b. Bortolotto could think quickly under pressure.

☐ c. The director should have taken better care of the YMCA building.

_____ Number of correct answers

Record your personal assessment of your work on the Critical Thinking Chart on page 150.

Summarizing and Paraphrasing

Follow the directions provided for questions 1 and 3. Put an X in the box next to the correct answer for question 2.

1. Look for the important ideas and events in paragraphs 10 and 11. Summarize those paragraphs in one or two sentences.

_____

_____

_____

_____

2. Below are summaries of the article. Choose the summary that says all the most important things about the article but in the fewest words.

☐ a.   When the ceiling collapsed at the YMCA in Roxbury, Massachusetts, lifeguard David Bortolotto helped to save children who were in the pool at the time.

☐ b.   When the ceiling collapsed at the YMCA in Roxbury, Massachusetts, employees risked their lives in order to save the children who were in the pool at the time.

☐ c.   When the ceiling collapsed at the YMCA in Roxbury, Massachusetts, nine children were in the pool learning how to swim. A lifeguard, David Bortolotto, immediately began to get the children out of the pool. The director of swim classes and the director of the YMCA also helped. Due to their quick actions, no one was killed.

3. Read the statement from the article below. Then read the paraphrase of that statement. Choose the reason that best tells why the paraphrase does not say the same thing as the statement.

Statement: [Bortolotto's] heart was racing too fast to feel the pain.

Paraphrase: The situation made his heart beat quickly.

☐ a.   Paraphrase says too much.

☐ b.   Paraphrase doesn't say enough.

☐ c.   Paraphrase doesn't agree with the statement from the article.

_____ Number of correct answers

Record your personal assessment of your work on the Critical Thinking Chart on page 150.

Critical Thinking

Put an X in the box next to the correct answer for questions 1 and 3. Follow the directions provided for questions 2, 4, and 5.

1. Which of the following statements from the article is an opinion rather than a fact?

☐ a.   Joyce rushed out of her office to see what was wrong.

☐ b.   One [parent] said she saw what looked like bits of confetti falling.

☐ c.   A few moments after everyone was out of the pool, a second section of roof came crashing down.

2. Choose from the letters below to correctly complete the following statement. Write the letters on the lines.

On the positive side, _____, but on the negative side _____.

a. several people were injured

b. a second section of the ceiling fell

c. no one was killed when the ceiling collapsed

3. What caused Bortolotto to look up at the ceiling?

☐ a. He heard a loud crack.

☐ b. He grabbed a child who was standing on the pool deck.

☐ c. He saw a piece of concrete falling from the roof.

4. In which paragraph(s) did you find the information to answer question 3? _____

5. Choose from the letters below to correctly complete the following statement. Write the letters on the lines.

According to the article, a collapsing ceiling caused _____ to _____, and the effect was that _____.

a. pull children out of the water

b. two lifeguards

c. no one was killed

_____ Number of correct answers

Record your personal assessment of your work on the Critical Thinking Chart on page 150.

Personal Response

I wonder why _____

_____

_____

_____

_____

Self-Assessment

From reading this article, I have learned _____

_____

_____

_____

_____

Compare and Contrast

Think about the articles you have read in Unit Three. Pick the three articles in which you thought people showed the most courage. Write the titles of the articles in the first column of the chart below. Use information you have learned from the articles to fill in the empty boxes in the chart.

Title	Who was courageous in this article?	What did this person/these people do to show courage?	What happened to this person/these people because of their actions?

Pick one of the articles in Unit Three. What would you have done if you were in the situation described in this article? _____

_____

_____

Words-per-Minute Table

Unit Three

Directions: If you were timed while reading an article, refer to the Reading Time you recorded in the box at the end of the article. Use this Words-Per-Minute table to determine your reading speed for that article. Then plot your reading speed on the graph on page 148.

Lesson No. of Words	11 1,082	12 838	13 1,120	14 1,102	15 930	
1:30	721	559	747	735	620	**90**
1:40	649	503	672	661	558	**100**
1:50	590	457	611	601	507	**110**
2:00	541	419	560	551	465	**120**
2:10	499	387	517	509	429	**130**
2:20	464	359	480	472	399	**140**
2:30	433	335	448	441	372	**150**
2:40	406	314	420	413	349	**160**
2:50	382	296	395	389	328	**170**
3:00	361	279	373	367	310	**180**
3:10	342	265	354	348	294	**190**
3:20	325	151	336	331	279	**200**
3:30	309	239	320	315	266	**210**
3:40	295	229	305	301	254	**220**
3:50	282	219	292	287	243	**230**
4:00	271	210	280	276	233	**240**
4:10	260	201	269	264	223	**250**
4:20	250	193	258	254	215	**260**
4:30	240	186	249	245	207	**270**
4:40	232	180	240	236	199	**280**
4:50	224	173	232	228	192	**290**
5:00	216	168	224	220	186	**300**
5:10	209	162	217	213	180	**310**
5:20	203	157	210	207	174	**320**
5:30	197	152	204	735	169	**330**
5:40	191	148	198	194	164	**340**
5:50	185	144	192	189	159	**350**
6:00	180	140	187	184	155	**360**
6:10	175	136	182	179	151	**370**
6:20	171	132	177	661	147	**380**
6:30	166	129	172	170	143	**390**
6:40	162	126	168	165	140	**400**
6:50	158	123	164	161	136	**410**
7:00	155	120	160	157	133	**420**
7:10	151	117	156	154	130	**430**
7:20	148	114	153	150	127	**440**
7:30	144	112	149	147	124	**450**
7:40	141	109	146	144	121	**460**
7:50	138	107	143	141	119	**470**
8:00	135	105	140	138	116	**480**

Minutes and Seconds

Seconds

Plotting Your Progress: Reading Speed

Unit Three

Directions: If you were timed while reading an article, write your words-per-minute rate for that article in the box under the number of the lesson. Then plot your reading speed on the graph by putting a small X on the line directly above the number of the lesson, across from the number of words per minute you read. As you mark your speed for each lesson, graph your progress by drawing a line to connect the X's.

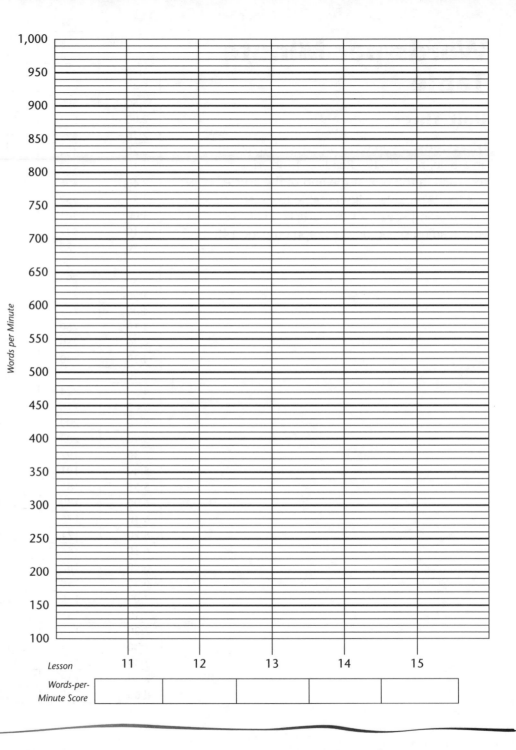

Words per Minute

Lesson: 11 12 13 14 15

Words-per-Minute Score

Plotting Your Progress: Reading Comprehension

Unit Three

Directions: Write your Reading Comprehension score for each lesson in the box under the number of the lesson. Then plot your score on the graph by putting a small X on the line directly above the number of the lesson and across from the score you earned. As you mark your score for each lesson, graph your progress by drawing a line to connect the X's.

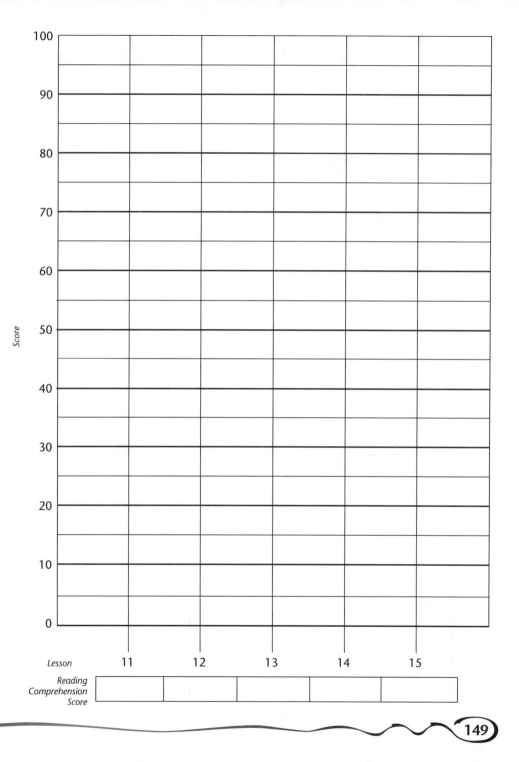

Plotting Your Progress: Critical Thinking

Unit Three

Directions: Work with your teacher to evaluate your responses to the Critical Thinking questions for each lesson. Then fill in the appropriate spaces in the chart below. For each lesson and each type of Critical Thinking question, do the following: Mark a minus sign (–) in the box to indicate areas in which you feel you could improve. Mark a plus sign (+) to indicate areas in which you feel you did well. Mark a minus-slash-plus sign (–/+) to indicate areas in which you had mixed success. Then write any comments you have about your performance, including ideas for improvement.

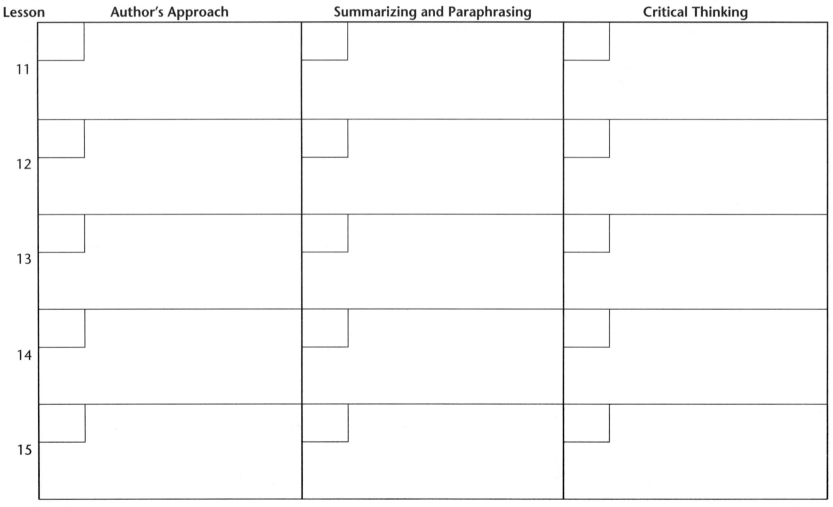

Lesson	Author's Approach	Summarizing and Paraphrasing	Critical Thinking
11			
12			
13			
14			
15			

Photo Credits